INTENTIONAL DADS

Insight into the Powerful Presence of Biological and Bonus Dads

by
Fa'Shay Halley

Watersprings
PUBLISHING

Intentional Dads published by Watersprings Publishing, a division of Watersprings Media House, LLC.
P.O. Box 1284 Olive Branch, MS 38654
www.waterspringspublishing.com

Contact the publisher for bulk orders and permission requests.

Printed in the United States of America.

Photography and Videography - The JNM Creative Agency, Jazzella McKeel - author back cover photo
Emazing Photography, Erica Daniels, About Author photo

Cover design - Fa'Shay Halley

ISBN-13: 979-8-9859594-7-5

Table of Contents

Special Acknowledgments

First, to the only "birth" Father I know, my AWESOME Heavenly Pops – thank you so much for your loving and consistent presence in my life. Thank you for ensuring that I never felt like a "fatherless" child, even though the world labeled me as such. Thank you for teaching me how to use the gifts and talents that you placed in me. No one could have ever told me that a young girl who couldn't read until 4th grade – the young lady who skipped English class regularly in high school out of fear that her poor reading and writing skills would be exposed, would one day be a woman who would write and publish a book. All I can say is that you continue to blow my mind and keep me in awe of what is possible when I partner with you. Thank You for blessing me with the BEST BONUS DADS EVER, as I know that each one of them was gifted to me by You!

Next, I would like to thank all my AMAZING bonus dads for investing in me with so much love and generosity. I am beyond grateful that you all answered the call to stand in the gap of my biological dad, whose identity is still unknown to me. Thanks for your INTENTIONAL presence! I will never be able to find adequate words to express my appreciation for the unconditional love and generous investments that each of you poured into me. But I pray you always remember that you hold a special place in my heart. Thanks again for stepping up and showing up for me. And most importantly, thank you for deciding to be vessels for the Lord to demonstrate His love through.

Finally, thank you to all the terrific biological and bonus dads who invested time to share insight about your fatherhood experiences with me. Thank you for being willing to be transparent and vulnerable during our "Straight Talk" interview sessions. There is no doubt that the insights you all shared will be a blessing to MANY!

Praises for Intentional Dads

What can be said about Fa'Shay Halley...?

She's funny and a believer in Christ. She is determined and is just a ray of sunshine. Last but not least, she's my wife! I'm happy to be the only one who can say that. And for the last twenty-two + years of our marriage, she has not deviated from the characteristics I just mentioned.

Her unique perspective toward all areas of life will undoubtedly challenge and change how you view things; this book is no exception. Fa'Shay will unapologetically tell you about her struggles and upbringing, and I assure you it will tug on your heart like a lovable character on a newly found show – but that is what this book is for!

Her story reads like a voyage through life, and along the way, she encounters her bonus dads and other individuals, whom she learns from and teaches them as well. I am blessed to have her in my life! And even though you're reading the cliffnotes version of her life, I believe you'll be blessed by it just as I have. Enjoy! - **Darrell Halley**

Living Testimony and Beneficiary of Intentional Father Figures...

I have known and loved Fa'Shay Halley her whole life as my god-sister, cousin, and one of my very best friends. Through our family ties and relationship, I have witnessed some of her turbulent childhood experiences firsthand. However, most importantly, I have had a front-row seat to her perseverance and ascension despite it all.

Her ability to make connections and adapt opened her up to receiving love, joy, protection, and support from many sources. This is evident in the relationships she cultivated with her bonus dads. They filled a void and had a tremendous impact on her life, inspiring this labor of love.

Fathers are an integral part of a child's development. Yes, they are needed monetarily, but they are also desired in so many other ways. Throughout the book, Fa'Shay discusses the importance of being an intentional dad in pursuit of modeling and developing emotionally healthy, secure, confident, and competent adults. She reminds us that this purposeful engagement should not be hindered but should be supported and always promoted. The shared personal stories and lessons learned illustrate that it's never too late to do better.

Fa'Shay is a living testimony and beneficiary of intentional father figures. She is beyond blessed, and I have no doubt she will bless others with her testimony and inspire dads along the way. - **Rekita Justice Logan**

Father, Dad, and Daddy...

I'm blessed to be able to say that I have had the privilege to build and maintain a relationship with my father, get to know my dad, and reap the benefits of being daddy's little girl. The world knows that it's impossible to have more than one biological father. But the world should also know that it's possible to have a father, a dad, and a daddy in our Heavenly Father.

My sister and friend, Fa'Shay, knows this firsthand. Her relationship with our Heavenly Father epitomizes a platonic relationship with pure intimacy. She's truly Daddy's little girl! Though He's not her biological father, He knew her before she was formed in her mother's womb. And the moment she understood who He was, they began this divine relationship, and she's never looked back. Whether she knows her biological father or not, she has/knows her Father, Dad, and Daddy in Our Heavenly Father. As you read this phenomenal book, I pray you are blessed to seek out our Father in Heaven, whether you know your biological father or not. - **Lisa N. Aldridge-Jones**

"A MAN NEVER STANDS AS
TALL AS WHEN HE KNEELS TO
HELP A CHILD."
- KNIGHTS OF PYTHAGORAS

Introduction

Before you dive into the pages of this book, I would like you to review and respond to the questions below:

1. Do you know who your biological dad is?
2. If you know who your biological dad is, do you have a healthy relationship with him?
3. Do you know someone who does not know who their biological dad is?
4. Do you know someone who has felt uncertain about their identity because they lacked a connection with their dad? – the someone might be you!

5. Do you know a dad who struggles with being present and available physically, mentally, emotionally, and/ or spiritually to their children? – this might also be you!
6. Have you heard someone spoken about as having 'daddy issues' – and it was implied that their 'daddy issues' impacted how they engaged in relationships?
7. Do you know someone who has been raised, mentored, or influenced by a male figure who was not their 'biological' dad?

If you are connected with any of the questions above – then I believe this book is for YOU!

Why I Wrote This Book

I wrote this book first and foremost as an appreciation tribute to my Heavenly Pops, my bonus dads, and other men I know who work fervently to be present and intentional fathers. After I decided to move forward with what I call one of my 'divine assignment,' I became more aware of how so many of us deeply connect through our life experiences, which creates opportunities for us to share and learn from one another. This is why I started the introduction with the questions I asked. I truly believe that most people can relate to some or all the questions through personal experience or by knowing someone else's experience. I also believe that our experiences (both direct and indirect) with our parents – dads and moms – play a significant role in how we engage in all our relationships – parental, platonic, romantic, etc. But because this book focuses on dads, we're going to spend most of our time on the powerful and generational impacts of their presence and absence. However, chapters five and six includes helpful insights for dads and moms. Please don't miss it.

In our world today, there seems to be an unsettling perception and growing narrative that says the presence of dads (biological or father figures – aka bonus dads) is no longer needed in the lives of children or the family construct. The message almost implies that a 'dad' is only 'nice to have' or 'optional' – which is far from true!

I firmly believe that intentional fathers are essential to everyone and in all aspect of life, and I am determined to use my voice and do whatever I can to improve the narrative of this topic. Trust me when I say that there is ABSOLUTELY NOTHING like having a man in your life who commits and is intentional about his role as a dad (biological or bonus). Having a dad who understands the importance of being present in a 'wholistic' and 'healthy' way – and doesn't allow his pride or other forces to convince him into thinking that he must be "perfect" to be present is invaluable. When men really start to understand how powerful their presence is and begin to embrace the role and responsibilities that can only be performed effectively by them – then they will be able to contribute to the ongoing growth and development of their child(ren) and the family unit, establishing a solid foundation for future generations.

Our world is in DESPERATE need of Intentional Dads! And to ensure we make the progress necessary for fruitful and sustainable change, it will take the INTENTIONAL partnership between dads and moms - co-parent partners. This is why I encourage both men and women to invest time in reading all of the insights shared in the chapters ahead. I truly believe that if you read with an open heart and a willingness to apply the insight shared, you will be moving in the right direction to help elevate this topic and improve your personal experiences.

What Is Covered in This Book

In summary, this book covers four primary points of view:

1. My testimony and personal view on how vital and beneficial I believe dads are in the lives of children, the family construct, the community, and the world. I'll share my exposure and experience of being blessed with the presence of intentional bonus dads, as well as the trauma of encountering a man who was ill-equipped to be a father figure in any capacity.
2. The current world view about the presence of dads in the lives of children.
3. The candid views on fatherhood come directly from dads.
4. The importance of co-parent partnerships.

In the sixth chapter, I extend a 'grace and growth' challenge to dads and moms, centered around choosing to do the 'personal' and 'partnership' work necessary to help our babies flourish.

My mom always taught me that everyone could 'bloom no matter where they were planted' – and my heart's desire is to encourage people to choose to bloom.

Resources To Enhance Your Reading Experience

This book contains various definitions, features, and insight reminders designed to enhance your growth experience. I encourage you to take some time to learn about the helpful resources, as they are designed to make your reading experience more engaging and practical.

In this section, you will find highlights on resources that have been included in the book to enhance your reading experience.

Chapter Insight Videos: I decided to use technology to our advantage to share brief insight videos at the beginning of each chapter. Viewing the chapter insight videos is simple. You can scan the QR code with your mobile device or go to my YouTube channel: Intentional Dads Movement, to access the chapter insight videos there.

Working Definitions: To ensure that we stay in sync, I've included 'working definitions' for keywords I will use. These words are very simple and typically used in everyday life. Still,

I've learned that communication is most effective when we invest time to level-set on definitions. Ensuring we have the same base meaning of a word helps mitigate confusion as we engage in conversations. Below are the working definitions:

- *Intentional Dad* - A man who deliberately and consistently engages in making investments that will nourish the 'complete' health and well-being of the children entrusted to him (i.e., spiritual, emotional, mental, and physical well-being). He is not "perfect," but he is present and in pursuit of developing and maintaining progressive relationships with his child(ren).
- *Biological Dad* – The father whose DNA a child carries.
- *Bonus Dad* – The father who is not biologically related to a child but provides for the child's needs or regularly cares for that child.
- *Co-Parent Partners* – Two individuals who share the responsibilities of raising a child. They are committed to partnering with one another to make the health and well-being of their child(ren) the primary focus.

Interviews: Chapter 3, "Straight Talk – No Chaser," is completely dedicated to sharing the questions and answers captured during interviews I conducted with men (biological and bonus dads) over a two-year period. I used the standard interview process, a structured question-and-answer conversation, and added post-interview call-to-action exercises. You'll learn more about it when you read Chapter 3, but know that the objective of this approach was to help initiate a dialog between dads and their children about perceptions verses realities of their relationship. The exercise was designed to help with narrative adjustments and encourage fruitful conversations. You'll definitely want to take the time to read all the questions and answers, as I learned so much from each dad simply by listening to their perspectives on the various topics discussed. I especially learned a TON when I asked how moms 'help and/or hinder' a dad's parenting efforts/experience. Again, I have NO DOUBT that the insights shared throughout this book will be valuable to you...as they certainly were helpful to me!

Encouragement Resources: At the end of the book, you will find a section titled "I.D. Encouragement Keys," which was included to share resources that I believe will nourish your soul. The resources shared offer loving reminders to help ignite the positive and progressive vibes you and your family will need. The section includes the following:

- Positive affirmations and a space for you to create your own
- Recommended song playlist – think of it as our I.D. Book Soundtrack
- Helpful book resources – which will be useful as you continue your growth journey

My prayer is that you allow yourself to 'truly' check out all of the resources shared and take in whatever you believe will benefit your 'personal' growth journey. I also hope that the resources provided encourage you to reconnect with your purpose and ignite an active passion inside you to never give up on working to become the best version of yourself in all roles that you're blessed with.

THANK YOU

Thank you in advance for investing in this resource and allowing it to be part of your 'personal' growth journey. The mere fact that you're reading this book and/or have decided to share it as a gift with someone else indicates that you're interested in growing and creating better experiences for yourself, your children, and others with whom you have relationships. The insight enclosed will not only help you gain additional perspective but also help you be an encouragement to other dads.

Special P.S.- To the moms and bonus moms investing time to read this book – THANK YOU! You are rare gems – and the world really needs you to continue to be refined and shine! Thank you for making such a significant investment that will benefit your growth journey as a mom and help you become more intentional about your contributions to your 'co-parenting partnership' and overall family dynamics.

Congratulations on making a personal level-up decision and progressing toward building strong relationships!

Much Love and Many Blessings Always,

Fa'Shay

"To be a great father
means being a great
listener. Your child's
emotions and thoughts
matter just as much as
your own."
- Denzel Washington

CHAPTER 1

It's Personal

"My story is filled with broken pieces, terrible experiences, and ugly truths. But it is also filled with major comebacks, meaningful relationships, many blessings, peace in my soul, and a grace that saved my life."
(Paraphrased & Personalized Quote from Arthur Holmer)

Background Perspective

To give you some perspective on how this book came to be, I would like to share some insight into what was happening when the Lord inspired me to write this book. In July 2019, my Raine family and I were working through the details of finalizing an intimate "celebration of life" for my first bonus dad, Tommy Raine Sr. Although I was on the emotional rollercoaster that comes with grief, I also felt immense gratitude. To be completely transparent, it felt odd to have such strong feelings of gratitude emerge while working through other tough emotions (i.e., sadness, confusion, disappointment, etc.). But every time I would think about what my bonus dad had to go through to maintain a connection with me and how his attitude was always jovial, even during a boatload of drama with my mom, it would shift my whole mood – from sadness to joy! The more I reminisced about our many 'daddy-daughter' moments, thee more my grief would subside, and I would find myself smiling, laughing, and saying – "My dad was such a huge and unapologetic goofball!" And if you know me, then you also know that I am a major goofball – unapologetically just like my bonus dad, which is one of the many reasons why our bond was so special.

Later in the book, I will introduce all my bonus dads, along with special impact memories of how their active presence helped to shape me into the woman I am today. But for now, I want to share a little bit more about my bonus dad, Tommy. So I don't confuse you, please note that I will refer to him as 'dad' throughout this chapter. I need to share a little more about how the Lord (who I refer to as my Heavenly Pops) used my dad's passing as a time to help me realize how blessed I was to have the presence of all my bonus dads. As I embraced every nostalgic moment – from our 'daddy-daughter' dates to all our favorite Seattle spots – Ivar's, Dick's, Taco Time, our motorcycle rides from Lake City to the Central District (CD) – I could clearly see my dad's intentional efforts to be present in my life. I also remembered some of our tough times when he and my mom didn't see eye to eye and when he was encountering his own struggles. Even during the turbulent moments we encountered, I could still see his unwavering love for me and his commitment to being as present as he could be. Each memory I recalled lifted my spirits, giving me exactly what I needed to begin my divine assignment in writing this book.

I thought about other significant aspects of our story, the huge decision he made as a young teenage man to be an 'active' dad. And even after learning that I was not his biological daughter, he was even more determined to ensure I remained connected to his family. Even shared his middle and last name with me – Dale and Raine.

My trip down memory lane helped me see how all of my bonus dads not only made the deliberate decision to serve as 'father figures' for me, but they also continued to make the decision to show up for me no matter what they had going on in their lives. As I mentioned during the introduction, I am not claiming that any of my bonus dads were perfect; I'm simply saying they were all perfect for me! I am also saying that I am more than confident that my Heavenly Pops orchestrated events that created the opportunity for each of them to serve as His earthly vessels to ensure I experienced His loving presence. For this, I will forever be grateful for my bonus dads' willingness to invest in my life and expand their family to include me.

This chapter is titled "It's Personal" because my passion for encouraging and nourishing progressive relationships is rooted in my personal experiences. The relationship between dads and their children and the dynamics between dads and moms (co-parent partnership) is very close to my heart. I know what it's like to have both 'healthy' and 'unhealthy' relationship exposure to father figures and co-parent partners.

My "Healthy" Exposure and Experience

Early in my life, I learned that establishing a stable foundation for anything you expected to grow – especially relationships was extremely important. In this section, we'll dive into more of my story and how not knowing my 'biological dad' afforded me the blessing of having ten father figures: one divine Father (My Heavenly Pops) and nine bonus dads. I'll also share how instrumental their INTENTIONAL presence was in establishing the fruitful foundation for me to grow and bloom!

As I mentioned earlier, a DNA test performed when I was a child revealed that Tommy Raine Sr. was not my biological father. After getting the results, my mom made sure I knew that he was not my father, but only when it was convenient for her. She was also transparent about the fact that she did not know who my biological dad was. My mom was unapologetically forthcoming with a lot of information she shared with me. Most people who know our journey would say the amount of transparency and exposure she extended to me was, at times, a little too much and unhealthy. And I would completely agree! I'm also positive she would say the same if she were still alive today. But being a young mother that didn't get to fully experience being parented by her mother or father, coupled with the immaturity of being a teenager and suffering unaddressed heart-wrenching trauma– she parented me the best way she could. As far back as I can remember, she didn't hold her tongue and was a 'what you see is what you get' kind of woman and mother. I share all this to say that I knew very early that Tommy Raine, Sr. was not my biological dad. But it wasn't a big deal to me because I never heard him say he wasn't, and he kept showing up for me. So, I sincerely never felt like I was lacking or "fatherless." However, I did feel special, kind of like he wanted to be my dad – and this made me feel like I was chosen!

Now, not knowing who my 'biological' dad was could have made it easy for me to feel like I was missing something. I could have accepted the "fatherless child" title and the various narratives that come with it. But I also learned early on that feeling incomplete and accepting titles or narratives that wouldn't serve me well would be counterproductive. I learned from many wise family members who poured into me that entertaining narratives that plant seeds of inadequacies, unworthiness, and an unhealthy amount of uncertainty would be toxic for me. So, they challenged me to explore and entertain thoughts that would encourage and empower me. Fortunately, my Heavenly Pops partnered with my bonus dads to create a powerful and purpose-filled narrative that still bears fruit in my life today.

Now, it's important for me to share that I also could have sabotaged the relationships with the Lord and my bonus dad, which would have created a different narrative and reality for me. If I opted to resist or not invest in the 'daddy-daughter' relationship and extended family relationships offered to me, there is NO DOUBT my life would be different. I wanted to call this out because my experiences also helped me learn about the power of reciprocity – "the practice of exchange with others for mutual benefits." I learned that relationships work best when there is a constant flow of reciprocity. I like to view reciprocity as an 'active' form of appreciation. It's a way to say, "I see and appreciate your investments in me, and in exchange, I will be equally invested." In my opinion, all healthy relationships require a constant flow of reciprocity – it's as vital as blood is to the body.

I've learned so many healthy and empowering lessons through my exposure and relationship experiences with my Heavenly Pops and bonus dads – that I decided to dedicate an entire chapter to highlighting them and my favorite lessons learned (Chapter 4 – Insight from a Grateful I.D. Beneficiary). So, I encourage you to keep reading because there is a lot more to share!

My "Unhealthy" Exposure and Experience

I haven't met a person yet who hasn't had some trauma or encountered difficult times in life. The details of our stories may differ, but most of us will agree that the impact of our personal experiences sometimes has a way of seeping into other areas of our lives. In this section, I will share how one of the darkest and most horrific experiences of my life almost sabotaged not only my relationships with my Heavenly Pops and bonus dads but also my overall perspective of men. The main character in this traumatic period was my mom's live-in boyfriend. The amount of trauma and dysfunction experienced during the time he was in my life is far too much to cover in this book, so I'm going to focus on sharing some of the counterproductive behaviors he demonstrated that could have been life-altering for me.

My mom's boyfriend was a man who was extremely self-absorbed and quick-tempered. In addition to these unhealthy tendencies, he desperately wanted to be revered as the head of our home. Still, he didn't contribute anything to it or take responsibility for leading in any capacity. Not only did he not want to invest in any household essentials, he didn't uplift my mom in any way or care about my well-being or growth. Unfortunately, my mom was with him for way too long – which means I had years of exposure and experience with a man who consistently demonstrated selfishness, immaturity, insecurity, and extreme violence. He was truly a horrible person, a terrible example of a man, and not even close to being able to serve as a father figure to me or anyone else – at least during the time he was in our lives.

Because of the length of time that my mom was with him, there were times that he felt like we (he and I) should be closer with some kind of 'daddy-daughter' bond or respect level, but that was absolutely not the case. I despised everything about him and couldn't see anything I could like or respect about him. I witnessed this man beat my mom in the face with a cowboy boot, slap the laughter out of her mouth, stomp her body into the corners of our apartments, and he spoke to her in ways that made her often seem like a frightened little girl. The only thing that kept me cordial with him was the basic lesson I was taught, which was to respect adults. However, there were times that I refused to show him respect because I honestly felt like he didn't deserve it.

I vividly recall one of the most traumatic days of my life. I was in either 2nd or 3rd grade, and I came home to my apartment building surrounded by police and an ambulance. Because of what had occurred before I went to school, I automatically knew that they were there attending to something at our apartment. But nothing could have prepared me for what I was about to walk into.

Early that morning, my mom begged me to miss school to stay home with her because her boyfriend had a bad attitude when he woke up. But I told her that I wanted to go to school because we were having a party. I remember walking to my bus stop that morning and debating with myself about feeling bad for not staying at home but also wanting to go to school and have fun. Even though I was pressed to go to school for some fun, I couldn't shake the feeling that I had in the pit of my stomach and the voice I had in my head that kept telling me something was wrong. I was full of anxiety the entire day and couldn't enjoy a moment of the party. Everything inside me told me that my mom needed me. I felt horrible and selfish simply because I opted to go to school. So, when my bus dropped me off at my stop, I ran as fast as I could home. And when I reached our apartment and saw all the emergency vehicles, my heart sank. At that moment, I told myself I had made the wrong decision by going to school.

The scene was so chaotic when I finally got to my building. Police and EMTs were focused on talking to potential witnesses and collecting evidence, so no one was monitoring who was coming in and out of the complex. My cousin lived in the apartment right under us on the first floor, and it's my understanding that a police officer was supposed to be on watch outside my apartment door so they could escort me to her when I got home from school. Unfortunately, that's not how it went down. While police officers were downstairs talking to my cousin my apartment door was cracked open and left unattended, with tape going across the door. So, I went under the tape and into a scene still burned in my mind to this very day. There was so much blood everywhere! I remember running through the apartment crying and screaming out for my mom, but only finding blood and furniture thrown all over the place. I finally entered the kitchen area, and that's when I saw glass everywhere. The entire window was gone, and that is when I completely broke down.

My cousin and the police rushed to me when they heard me and took me out of the apartment. My cousin then told me that my mom's boyfriend had beat her up and pushed her out the window of our two-story apartment. And it was at that moment that my heart was completely hardened towards him, and he became my #1 enemy. An enemy I was also determined to hurt as soon as I could work up enough courage and had the right opportunity.

And guess what? The day of 'courage and opportunity' came a year or so later. I remember it like it was yesterday. We lived in a project complex called Springwood not too far outside Seattle, WA. A few friends came to get me from the playground to let me know that my mom was getting beat up by her boyfriend (AGAIN). So, I ran home full of rage, and when I entered the apartment, I went through the kitchen to grab a knife. I had already decided that day I would commit to doing what I felt I had to do to protect us. Of course, I didn't think my plan through or know exactly what I was walking into. By the time I got to the backyard, where he had her, the police had arrived. And when they arrived, I still had the knife in my hand. As some officers were handcuffing him and he continued with his vicious threats, other officers were trying to calm me down and asked me to drop the knife, and my mom was also begging me to do the same. Although I heard the officers, I really zoned in on my mom's distress. With the knife still in my hand, I told her I needed to protect us because he wouldn't ever stop. She continued crying and pleading with me, and she promised it was over. She said that she was finally done with him. So, I dropped the knife, and she kept her promise.

The next day, we left EVERYTHING we had (i.e., clothes, shoes, family pictures, furniture, TVs, etc.). We had been through this same routine several times before leaving everything behind, only to have him be released shortly after because she failed to press charges. He would then come by wherever we were staying and reel her back in – and the dysfunctional cycle would continue. But this time was different! This time, she located various 'women's safe houses' across Seattle's Central District and asked if we could stay a night or two. When that wasn't possible, we would visit local shelters to check for openings. And there were a couple of times when we couldn't find a 'safe house' or 'shelter,' so my mom would find other inconspicuous places for us to sleep, like under the staircase of a secured apartment building in what she felt was a safe neighborhood.

So, my mom did whatever she could to keep us moving. I believe she did this because she knew she had to safeguard herself from getting caught up again. She knew that once her boyfriend got released from jail, that he would start showing up at the same spots she would be. I believe that in an effort to keep her promise to me, she made a choice to do something different. She made a choice to take what I'm sure was a scary leap of faith to seek help from outside of her normal support circle – and definitely outside of her comfort zone.

When she finally let our family know everything that was going on and how we were surviving – just like any supportive family would do when someone is 'truly' ready to change their life – they opened their homes and hearts and protected us the best way they could. Even though we faced more rough terrain on our journey ahead – I would say the darkest time of my life was over. Occasionally, I think about how my life could've turned out so differently if my mom had decided to keep us in that abusive and dysfunctional cycle. This leads me to sometimes think about if I were experiencing the same chaos and trauma as a child in today's time, and I responded in the way I did to protect my mom and me from an abuser. I may not even be alive right now. I'm not insinuating that my actions were right; I'm simply saying that I know that fear and desperation to be free from abuse can result in life-altering changes for the person being abused, the child witnessing the abuse, and all of those around them.

Fortunately, after this tragic part of my story concluded, I could still appreciate the presence of men in a healthy way. I even picked up a few extra bonus dads after this tragic chapter of my life. I'm so grateful that even though my mom's boyfriend's deeply-rooted 'insecurities and trauma' created 'trauma and insecurities' in me – they didn't override the 'positive' influences in my life. So, I can say now: THANK THE LORD for His presence, my bonus dads, and others that helped me see men differently – because I would have been lost without them.

I sometimes laugh at the fact that I have so many bonus dads – as I shared, I have a total of nine. But I truly believe that the impact of encountering that 'one' HORRIBLE man required a LOT of work for me to heal and extend trust to men again. I think the Lord said, "My baby-girl needs some extra reinforcement," – and he sure did a PHENOMENAL job selecting the perfect bonus dads for me!

Acknowledgment and Healing

Acknowledging and addressing my mom's contributions to the dysfunction and trauma I experienced was no easy task. Whenever I share parts of my story, people will sometimes ask why I wasn't mad at my mom for what she did or did not do to protect me. I completely understand the question and where they're coming from because I've asked myself the same question many times. I believe I became my mom's protector because I felt she was in distress. Like most kids in my situation, since my mom needed my help and protection, I did not want to do anything that made her feel worse. Although,

I didn't understand why she wasn't protecting herself when I knew she could. It didn't stop me from wanting to protect her.

Unfortunately, I didn't realize how fierce and counter-productive my need to 'protect' her would become. I also didn't realize how my need to protect and rescue her would begin to seep into other areas of my life in very unhealthy ways. Because we operated in this dysfunctional space for so long, she became comfortable with me operating in a protective role, and I also felt most comfortable in that space. Throughout most of our life together, we operated in a 'parent-child role reversal' situation –formally known as 'parentification.'

> ## PARENTIFICATION:
> A role reversal between parent and child. A child's personal needs are sacrificed in order to take care of the needs of the parent(s).
> *(Source: NewportAcademy.com)*

I share this simply because it was hard for us to see our relationship's reality – because we were in it. It was even more challenging for me to fathom the idea that it was not my responsibility to be the protector. To be completely transparent, it took quite a bit of counseling and coaching with wise individuals (including some of my bonus dads and my husband) to deal with the various layers of dysfunction. But it all paid off, as the help I received enabled me to address every single one of my experiences and concerns with her directly. I could also share with her what I felt about her contributions and the impact on me and our relationship. Once again, addressing the topics head-on was tough, but I would do it all again because it helped us both heal and grow. Our many crucial conversations (e.g., engaging in a dialog when the stakes are high, emotions are high, but you need to preserve the relationship.) helped us learn that 'problems don't age well.' We learned that it is best to do whatever we can to acknowledge and address issues immediately, leveraging professional resources appropriately.

Learning to share my experiences with transparency and unapologetically was liberating, humbling, and empowering!

I'm definitely happy that my mom and I sought out counseling and coaching. Learning to be transparent and unapologetic was liberating, humbling, and empowering. It also helped me 'see me,' which has been extremely valuable in all of my relationships. I can honestly say at one point in my life, I was nervous about whether I could ever maintain a 'healthy' romantic relationship. I didn't want to continue the cycle I had been exposed to (e.g., chaos, dishonesty, abuse, manipulation, etc.). It was clear that all relationships took work and that no one was perfect – but I just wasn't sure how to stop my past from infecting my future. I certainly did not want to subject a child to any drama I experienced. So, again, counseling and coaching were not a 'luxury' for me; they were 'necessities.'

They truly helped me work through a lot of the baggage I didn't want to carry with me any longer.

There is NO DOUBT that the investments made in my life have birthed a personal passion that helps me be more intentional in all of the roles I serve in – as a daughter, wife, mother, friend, and servant-leader in corporate America and my community.

Who knows, perhaps one day I'll share more details about my life journey experiences, but until then, I'll conclude with one of my favorite quotes – paraphrased and personalized:

"One day, I will tell my story of how I've overcome what I went through, and it will become part of someone else's survival and thrive guide."
        – Personalized and Paraphrased by Brené Brown

In closing, I would like to implore parents (dads and moms) to please remember these key points -

- Allowing your child(ren) to have harmful exposure and experiences through your lifestyle can result in life-altering impacts.
- Be careful of who you are in a relationship with – everyone does not have the character or maturity to be around your children, no matter how much you like/ love them.

■ One traumatic experience has the power to cast negative and dark shadows over other relationships – even the positive ones.

Once we have children, they must be our primary priority. Protecting and nourishing their growth, in every way must be at the top of our priority list – period! I get that we (parents) also need to invest in ourselves and other adult relationships, but not at the expense of our children. We must ensure that our efforts to keep our lives 'lit' don't jeopardize or burn out the 'lights' in our children.

The bottom line is that as parents, we have a responsibility to acknowledge all things that could be counterproductive to the health and well-being of our children and us. Anything or anyone that we're investing in or entertaining that is not contributing to the relationship with our kids in a fruitful manner must be released or regulated (i.e., no access or strict boundaries).

Again, the relationship dynamics between co-parent partners (dads and moms) and children are very personal, and I share more insight on this topic in Chapters 5 and 6. Just know that the parental points outlined above are valuable lessons learned from my exposure and experiences, and they are very close to my heart. So, I hope you decide to truly ponder what I shared, acknowledge 'personal' growth opportunities, and choose to adopt lessons learned to help restore and/or strengthen your relationships.

"WHAT COMES FROM THE HEART
GOES TO THE HEART."
– SAMUEL TAYLOR COLERIDGE

"Show your children the power of love and forgiveness. They will carry these lessons with them throughout their lives and pass them on to their own children."
- Morgan Freeman

CHAPTER 2

Addressing and Adjusting the Fractured Father Image

"A good father is one of the most unsung, unpraised, unnoticed, and yet one of the most VALUABLE assets in our society."

– Billy Graham

Narrative Adjustment Required

There is a great need for fathers in our world today. Mothers need them, children need them, and our community needs them. But for reasons beyond my comprehension, there is an unsettling narrative that seems to permeate every aspect of the world. The primary message of this counterproductive narrative is that men/fathers are no longer needed to contribute to the family unit. This narrative is not only false but also extremely damaging to our society. We need a serious narrative adjustment – and we need it now! So, let's continue exploring areas that need to be addressed to begin our work.

Have you ever taken the time to think about some of the counterproductive perceptions about fathers in our society? It seems as though the adoration and respect for fathers shared by past generations are diminishing. As I conducted interviews with men about fatherhood, I learned that men of all races, cultures, social classes, economic statuses, and faith backgrounds also felt that there was a shift in how their presence and contributions were valued in today's world.

Below are a few common generalized perspectives shared about men and fatherhood that I would say are counterproductive and not always true about men/fathers-

- Fathers are not capable or interested in providing children with mental, emotional, and spiritual guidance/support.
- Fathers are irresponsible and cannot be depended on to provide the level of nurturing and discipline a child needs.
- Fathers are not interested in being engaged in their children's lives unless it involves something that piques their interest.
- Fathers are no longer needed in the family construct or child-rearing process. Instead, women can serve as moms and dads, providing for all children's needs.
- The presence of the father is 'optional' in a child's life – and his absence will not have much impact on the child's growth and development.

- Fathers who cannot provide all the financial support requested or desired to add value to a child's life.
- Fathers are not present in their children's lives because they choose not to be.

These are just a few basic comments shared that were mentioned not only about men/fathers in the US but also in other countries. To be completely honest, I know some of these statements to be true for some fathers, but it doesn't hold true for a lot of the men I know.

But since we're talking about it – can you think of the men you know these statements would be true for? If so, whether they are true for you or someone you know – have you ever challenged yourself and others to answer questions like –

- Is this the narrative you want to be aligned with your legacy?
- How do one or all of these statements show up in your life, and how did they start?
- What can you do to begin improving the narrative?

If you haven't asked yourself these questions - it's all good! Today is the day you can explore each question and commit to being more intentional about making a 'personal' investment towards elevating narratives and experiences. If you need help to sort through your thoughts, evaluate your relationships, and make a 'practical' action plan – I believe some of the insight shared in the pages and chapters ahead will be extremely useful. As I shared in the previous chapter,

I'm an advocate of pursuing wise counseling and coaching professionals for anyone who truly desires to progress in areas involving trauma, deeply rooted issues, etc. Since we cannot see ourselves from an outside perspective, it can sometimes be challenging to have a clear perspective of ourselves without conferring with others. Please be sure the person you consult with has a good balance of 'courage' and 'compassion' – because we all need people around us who can both lovingly connect and course-correct us when it's necessary.

"If you have more people around you who care about your character rather than your comfort – you are RICH indeed."
– Unknown

We Need to See and Hear You

The narrative about the contributions and value that men/fathers add to the family unit and in our communities will only improve when we begin to hear and see men/fathers of all backgrounds consistently present – and actively engaged. I'm convinced that most men/fathers don't know how much power and influence they have been equipped with, either because of a lack of awareness or inability to properly use what they have. There are some men who don't believe they have what it takes to be an intentional dad. However, I'm positive that if they invested time to learn how to operate in their God-given role and initiate uncomfortable conversations, they would see who they are capable of being. Most fathers just need to commit to doing the challenging work required to improve their narratives. That is when progressive changes manifest in their relationships and experiences.

Contrary to what the world may say today, men/fathers were divinely gifted to lead, protect, provide (not only financially), heal, encourage, and so much more. Some of the greatest mental and emotional issues that people suffer from are those neglected areas by fathers/men who were designed to provide those attributes. Before anyone gets the wrong idea, I also hold the belief that women/mothers bring their own distinct essence to raising children. The core of my argument is that disregarding the importance of children being exposed to and benefiting from the inherent nurturing abilities of both men/dads and women/moms is detrimental to all of us.

Our children, women/moms, and the world desperately need men/fathers – and we always will. We need them to willingly put all pride to the side and unapologetically demonstrate authenticity, vulnerability, transparency, humility, forgiveness, grace, and maturity. Our world needs to see men/fathers address some of the uncomfortable issues that are becoming plagues in our families and communities today. We need to know that we can count on our men/fathers to show up and fight for relationships and families - no matter what!

During my interviews with some of the fathers, it was clear to me that they desired to be everything their children needed and wanted. Still, their internal strongholds were getting in the way of them being who they desperately wanted to be. A few even implied that displaying vulnerability might exhibit a level of weakness. But they also acknowledged that being transparent and vulnerable would help them address some of the roadblocks they faced, like shame, inadequacies, trauma, unforgiveness, etc. As I processed the shared stories and thoughts, it became clear that some men don't even realize that it takes an immense amount of 'strength' to authentically display vulnerability, especially when it comes to making personal improvements. The word 'vulnerability' has been misinterpreted and turned into a derogatory term. It is viewed as an act of weakness – which is far from true. The truth is that demonstrating vulnerability is one of the most courageous things anyone can do – especially men/fathers.

How powerful would it be if our men/fathers decided to become more comfortable and confident with operating in the strength of vulnerability?

How amazing would it be if our men/fathers decided to consistently demonstrate their servant-leadership through a healthy balance of vulnerability, wisdom, maturity, and loving masculinity?

I'm absolutely convinced that our men/fathers across the globe can be the men/fathers our world so desperately needs today. They just have to be committed to doing their personal work from the inside out.

Man Behind the Mask

We need more men/fathers to begin initiating and engaging in meaningful dialogue centered around – the need/value of their presence, the impact of their absence, and roadblocks that are preventing them from building healthy relationships. When these meaningful conversations start to flow, so does healing and restoration. But in order for these meaningful conversations to take place, we'll first have to address the 'masks' that many men/fathers wear. The masks that prevent them from addressing the real issues. The masks that keep counterproductive perceptions, narratives, and experience masquerades in motion.

Before we get too deep into this topic, let's acknowledge that most people opt to 'wear a mask' instead of allowing their true selves to be seen by others, especially in this social media world we live in today. Let's also acknowledge that some people don't wear a mask for clout; Some opt to wear it when they feel the need to safeguard themselves.

We all have a tendency to slap our masks on when we are -

- Uncomfortable being transparent and vulnerable because we are apprehensive about the emotions we may experience or display.
- Uncertain about how others will receive us if we are fully transparent and vulnerable.
- Unfamiliar with those around us, so we've decided to allow our 'masked' representative to take center stage

until we become more familiar with whom we're dealing with.

I'm providing this prelude to acknowledge that no one is exempt from 'wearing a mask' from time to time – but it becomes an issue when the mask prevents us from 'knowing' and 'growing' the person behind the mask.

In this section, I want to take some time to talk about why our children, women, and the world need to see the men/ fathers behind the masks. We need to see them walk courageously and unapologetically in who they are. We need to see them address areas of their lives that are not only holding them captive and stunting their growth but also hindering all those connected to them.

As mentioned before, many men would agree that they wear their masks mostly when emotional topics come up that might reveal a level of vulnerability. If topics come up that trigger memories of trauma or difficult times, some men don't put on masks; they just disengage, disconnect, or shut down completely. Again, our personal growth goal as 'maturing' adults is to become more self-aware. If there are areas in our lives not serving us or our loved ones 'well,' it would be in our best interest to become more aware of what we can and cannot do so our efforts are more fruitful.

Since "we" are truly everywhere "we go" and can't ever really escape ourselves – it's important to invest time in getting more acquainted with ourselves. Some questions that we should ask ourselves include:

- Are you comfortable with demonstrating emotions?
- Do you feel uncomfortable or exposed when emotions are triggered by or in front of others?
- Do you feel the need to safeguard yourself from others?
- Are you good at putting up protective walls to keep people from getting too close?
- Do you become defensive, angry, passive, or deflect when topics come up that may trigger your emotional memories?

We need men/fathers to challenge themselves to answer these questions honestly and challenge others, especially if we desire to see the men behind the mask.

Throughout my life, I've heard so many guys express that one of the most challenging things for them to do authentically is to share and demonstrate a 'healthy' amount of emotions. This can be such a challenge for them to effectively express. However, it can be even more challenging to teach their children how to process, manage, and share emotions. Again, I'm not saying that only men/fathers experience this challenge. I just would like to zone in a little more on our men/dads for now. But rest assured that I have more insight to share with my fellow women/moms in the chapters to come.

The bottom line is that some of the counterproductive narratives that exist today about men/fathers will require all men/fathers to initiate and engage in candid conversations on topics to address what is really going on the inside of men/fathers, such as:

- What mental/emotional strongholds exist? What resources do they need to help them grow and be empowered? What's the best way to support them, etc.?
- What do children need and want from the men/fathers in their lives?
- What do mothers/women need from the men/fathers in their lives?
- What do men/fathers need from other men/fathers who have learned how to improve their lives and the lives of their loved ones?

When men/fathers avoid topics about unresolved issues and refuse or reject resources that can help on a path toward healing and growth, they are doing a disservice to themselves and their children, co-parent partners, and communities. The world needs men/fathers across the globe to become more intentional about investing and embracing their own healing! It is truly the only way we'll begin to experience the powerful, fruitful, and sustainable change we desperately need.

"Of all the rocks upon which we build our lives, we are reminded today that family is the most important. And we are called to recognize and honor how critical every father is to that foundation. They are teachers and coaches. They are mentors and role models. They are examples of success and the men who constantly push us toward it. But if we are honest with ourselves, we'll admit that what too many fathers also are is missing – missing from too many lives and too many homes. They have abandoned their responsibilities,

acting like boys instead of men. And the foundation of our families are weaker because of it."

– President Barak Obama – Father's Day Speech,
Politicio, June 15, 2008

Remember, we can't be the best examples, teachers, coaches – and, most importantly, parents if we're unwilling to be present, responsible, and committed to the growth of ourselves and others. How our kids experience us daily influences their narrative about what men/dad, women/mom, co-partner partners, family, and home really are. The concept of "each one teach one" will happen one way or another – the question is, what are we teaching, intentionally and unintentionally?

I won't get into all of the research and statistics about this topic because the bottom line is that our children learn the fundamentals of parenting, family, and relationships at home. This is important for us (parents) to remember because it will be difficult for us to provide them with the examples and insights needed to develop strong and flourishing relationships with our children. We must consistently practice being present, engaged, honest, communicative, vulnerable, forgiving, grateful, and willing to give grace in order to become good at it!

Again, once something is experienced, it's easier for us to share it with others with more confidence and compassion – resulting in stronger connections with those around us. And I believe that as more men/fathers work to grow and become more comfortable with who they are on a 'spiritual, emotional, and mental' level, the more confident they will be in allowing others to experience the unmasked version of themselves.

Today, more than ever, we need men/fathers to be unapologetic about investing in their personal healing and growth process. It truly doesn't do anyone any good if they are out here putting up a front – and acting like things are all good when they are not.

I don't know if you all remember the old-school song by MC Breed called *Ain't No Future in Yo Frontin*. The title always stuck with me because I felt it was simple and direct. It reminded me that there was no 'real' future in investing in disguises because it was not sustainable, as life has a way of always revealing what is 'real' and what is a 'facade.' Now, I know most of you will probably go and listen to the song again and say, "Shay, this song message was not totally connected with your message!" My response is, "I know!" but I'm a person who LOVES music. Sometimes, when I listen to lyrics, I ponder them through my 'practical life application' lenses – and well, they end up sticking with me – LOL. I think it would be beneficial for you to allow this song title to stick with you, too.

'Fronts' or facades do not have a sustainable future – and are never a healthy way to lead or engage in relationships, especially when it comes to teaching and being an example for our kids or partnering with someone else to raise our children.

Learning how to operate in life and engage with others authentically will not only help you become more confident in your own skin but will also help your relationships with your children and co-parent partners. Since many men/dads find it challenging to express or be exposed to situations that could trigger emotions, including – insecurities, fear, rejection, failure, shame, etc. – it can also result in triggering 'self-protection' alarms. When 'self-protection' alarms are triggered, safety is questioned, walls come up, and masks are put on. Unfortunately, when you put on your masks to avoid areas that you know need improvement, you stunt your growth, and your relationships suffer. You also continue to feed into the counterproductive narrative about men/fathers instead of being part of the solution. Wearing masks, investing in facades, and being evasive will only produce surface connections that are not fruitful or sustainable.

Again, even though our focus is on men/dads, as shared before, most of this insight also applies to me and my fellow women/moms. The bottom line is that our children will need both parents to put in some major work as individuals and partners – especially if we want our kids to have an opportunity to experience the best version of us. Again, our primary focus must be on doing our 'personal' work, partnering to improve the experiences of our children and elevate narratives about men/fathers in a more positive and productive way. It's time to be intentional about the way we live life. The best place to start is by refusing to wear masks and committing to seeing and sharing the "true" version of yourself.

Unlocking the Shackles of Shame

As I mentioned several times, I had the privilege of spending quality time with dads to discuss their experiences with fatherhood. Something I found surprising is the amount of time I spent with each of them. I only planned to spend an hour for each interview, assuming that I could cover all the questions I had during that time. I subconsciously thought the men would share 'concise' responses, especially since I provided them with the questions before our meeting.

Until I conducted these interviews, I had not encountered many men who would voluntarily spend a long time engaging in dialogue that could trigger emotions. But, to my surprise, the time flew by once the dads started sharing their experiences. So, what was only supposed to be an hour at the most ended up being a couple of hours, and some interviews were even longer.

During the interview process, I noticed a recurring theme about the topic of 'shame.' The dads spent a good deal of time sharing how some situations they encountered brought up a lot of mixed emotions – and shame was at the top of their list. Several dads expressed that their experience with shame was either related to failures or missed opportunities. They also shared that the shame they struggled with started in one area of their lives but found a way of impacting other parts of their lives. It was as if the shame they felt was holding them hostage. Even in instances where they believed they could possibly do something to reduce the amount of shame they felt, the fear of conflict and rejection emerged, making it hard for them to address the situation head-on.

Some of the examples of how shame and fear impacted their lives included:

- Their personal growth and confidence as men, fathers, and leaders.
- Their ability to develop and maintain productive and growing relationships with some or all their kids (children and adults).
- Their ability to effectively engage, navigate, and sustain healthy romantic and platonic relationships.
- Their ability to bridge gaps that separated them from having healthy relationships with their parents and other relatives.

After hearing these dads share their hearts, it became abundantly evident to me that it was time to make major adjustments. Their stories further emphasized why more open and candid conversations addressing the real feelings and fears that men/dads face are mission-critical to everyone. It was clear that men/dads would have to commit to working on their own *'shame release plan'* in order to experience healthy and sustainable changes they desired in relationships. The relationships with their children and co-parent partners had to be their primary priority. The interviews also revealed that now is the time for co-parent partners (dads and moms) to develop a unified approach to the healing and family unit, covered more in chapters five and six. The bondage created by shame may start in one person or area but eventually seeps into the lives of everyone around them, which is why addressing and healing internal issues is not an 'individual' crisis – it's a family, community, and world crisis.

During the interviews, I learned that most of the issues and battles the dads were dealing with (internally and externally) were not discriminatory. The issues and challenges experienced crossed all races, countries, age groups, faith affiliations, and social and economic statuses. One of the toughest areas they said was difficult to overcome was their thoughts and the emotional conflicts they experienced daily. So, I worked really hard to be mindful to create a space of peace and comfort during every interview. Every dad I spoke with seemed ready and willing to be open and transparent during our interview process, which made my heart smile.

The strength and courage each dad demonstrated as they seized the opportunity to share their experience with vulnerability and transparency inspired me. The more we talked about specific situations that were linked to the feelings of 'shame' and 'hopelessness' the more I could also see sparks of empowerment and optimism, not by anything I did but through their ability to embrace the moment and demonstrate courage to deal with the emotions that they would typically avoid. It was as if they became encouraged the more they talked through some of the situations. It was as if they started to entertain the possibility of being released from the narratives that weighed heavy on their hearts and minds. Again, I don't have the right words to adequately describe how amazing it was to share these transformational moments with the dads, but know that it was beyond special!

These experiences further emphasized why it is so important for dads/men to be more deliberate about investing in their own mental and emotional well-being. Today, more than ever, many things can create roadblocks and disconnects in our relationships. These disconnects and roadblocks prevent us from establishing a healthy view of ourselves and others. They can prevent us from addressing issues, and trauma that still holds us captive, as well as stunts our growth process. Unfortunately, if we don't intentionally deal with the situations we know exist, we can unintentionally pass all our "mess" to our children and others.

IT STARTS WITH YOU

So, my questions to every dad/man are - "Are you good with adversely affecting your children and the relationship you have with them? Are you good with passing life-altering or threatening ailments to your children, family, and community when you know that you have the ability to stop them from being infected?

If your answer is no – "I don't want to negatively impact the 'spiritual, emotional, mental, or physical' well-being of my children and family. I do want to find ways to deal with my situations so that I can be more of who I am purposed to be for me, my children, and anyone I encounter." Then, the wonderful news is you can start today!

There is an 'active' battle taking place in the minds of men/dads today, along with constant emotional conflicts in their hearts! These battles and conflicts must be addressed head-on for 'true' progress and freedom to be experienced.

If you are not *intentional* about seeking out ways to address these internal battles, you will remain imprisoned and unable to extend the emotional support that your children and families need.

The AWESOME news is that there are resources available and designed to help you begin unpacking all the situations weighing heavy on you so that you can begin the healing process. These same resources can also help you identify and remove roadblocks preventing you from properly nurturing the relationships that matter most to you. If you want to learn about ways and resources you can leverage to make improvements personally and in your relationships, the best place to start is a professional counselor who aligns with your belief system. I've learned from personal experience that finding the 'right' resource will take some effort, but it's worth it! I've also learned that there is a ton of easily accessible, no-cost, or low-cost 'quality' counseling/coaching available; I just had to be willing to ask for help and do the work.

Remember, *you* can become the best version of yourself – no matter what you've done or been through! As the 'co-author' of your life story, you have also been granted authority to adjust the narrative at any time during your journey.

Make a U-Turn!

Today can be the day that you decide to begin a new chapter! Heck, you can even start a whole new book if you want to! Just decide to do something daily that will help create the legacy you want to leave behind.

Please remember that when you decide to do something 'new,' it may feel uncomfortable initially. Some of your past thoughts and actions may try to push their way into your 'revised' narrative – which is normal. No one is exempt from the challenges experienced during a transitional period. Personally, I call these periods my 'wilderness experiences.' I refer to these in this way because I believe, at times, we act like the children of Israel when they were freed from bondage and were headed to the Promised Land. They found themselves on an extended journey, 40 years in the wilderness, trying to shake their self-sabotaging and tendencies. My point is that we're all human, which means we can sometimes wander in the same place and also operate in our self-sabotaging ways for years – but we don't have to! We can choose to acknowledge and address our situation and make the changes necessary to get back on track. Then, we can build a legacy full of purpose, power, and promise!

Dads, NOW is the time! Today is the day for you to decide to commit to investing in your 'personal' growth so that you can share the best version of yourself with your children and others you have relationships with.

Your legacy work must begin NOW!

If you want to be in your children's memories tomorrow, you MUST be in their lives today!

- You don't want to miss the opportunity to have a 'lead' role in your child(ren)'s life.
- You don't want to miss the privilege of inspiring and influencing their narratives.
- You want your children to know that you were committed to becoming the best version of yourself so that you can help them discover and develop the best version of themselves.
- You want to show them how to intentionally invest in a personal healing process by acknowledging and addressing all issues that prevent you from growing so that you can be available to them spiritually, mentally, emotionally, and physically.
- You want your child(ren) to know that even if you've missed out on some of the chapters of their lives, you are committed to being present and active now.

Practice makes progress...and *consistent* practice creates permanence!

As we close this chapter, always remember:

- Dads are more than just the sum of their parts and their financial/tangible contributions – their presence provides nourishment and security to the hearts and souls of the family.

- The value of a present, loving, and intentional dad is priceless!
- You are empowered to adjust the narratives of your own story – and you should, especially if it can help you and your family heal and progress.
- Narratives are not always easy to adjust when it comes to others' perceptions of you – but it's all good! Be patient, extend yourself and others' grace, and stay the course!
- Intentional dads are truly INVALUABLE – and immensely needed in our world today!

Dads, you have what it takes to elevate the current 'fractured' father image and experience. Know that practice makes progress, and *consistent* practice creates permanence. So, commit to your growth journey and always practice being intentional, authentic, vulnerable, transparent, forgiving, gracious, and courageous!

"Courage starts with showing up - and letting ourselves be seen."
- Brené Brown

CHAPTER 3

Straight Talk– No Chaser

"Courage is contagious. When brave men take a stand, the spines of others are often shifted."

– Billy Graham

The dads I had the privilege of interviewing made this chapter a MUST-read! Whether you decide to read the questions and answers in the order I asked them or skip around to read them based on your specific interest, I believe that you will be enlightened by the insight shared.

Interview Background and Demographics

Before we dive into the 'Straight Talk' Q&A details, it's important to provide you with some general information about my interview participants. Below are some general demographic details about the dads I had the pleasure of interviewing:

- **Race:** African American, Native American Mix, White-American, Greek, Zimbabwean, and Multi-Raced; some men were from the US, and others were from other countries.
- **Dad's age:** Participants' ages range from 30s – early 70s.
- **Fatherhood status:** Biological Dads, Bonus Dads (i.e., stepdad, foster dad, etc.) or both.
- **# of Children:** 1 – 5: One interview participant not only had four children of his own, but he and his wife also had over 50 foster children through the years, whom they still have good relationships with today.
- **Age ranges of the dad's children:** 8 years old to mid-40s, and several have grandchildren.
- **Genders of their children:** Varied; some had a mix, while others had all boys or all girls.
- **Relationship status:** Men who were married, divorced, or single.
- **Faith affiliation:** Christian, Catholic, Agnostic, Atheist, Non-denominational/Religious, God-fearing, and Spiritual.

This diverse participant base made the interview experience unique and rich! The diversity also made it clear to me that the dads shared common experiences. Acknowledging this helped me realize that the 'daddy wounds' that many people experience also span across every race, culture, and region of the world. This also means that if we begin working together to encourage dads/men to do their 'personal' work and dads/moms could work together to improve their co-parenting partnerships, then we could start to heal 'daddy-wounds' – and begin experiencing 'daddy-blessings,' which is what we all need in our world today!

Investing the time to learn more about how men experienced fatherhood was definitely an eye-opening and humbling experience for me as a woman. My initial intent for the book was to create a special recognition for my bonus dads and celebrate all of the 'intentional dads.' What I didn't realize was that the Lord had a different plan – that included more layers and time.

The time I invested in conducting the interviews not only helped me with the completion of my divine assignment (this book) but also helped me grow as a woman, wife, mother, sister, daughter, and friend. I feel like my overall listening and communication skills also improved through this experience. I was challenged in many ways during this process, especially when I interviewed men I didn't know well. I can honestly say I didn't expect the dads to share so many details, so I was pleasantly surprised. Each time I concluded an interview, I was inspired and immensely grateful for the investment of time and the experiences shared by each dad.

*Note: The information shared does not represent the thoughts of all the dads interviewed or all men. However, it does provide insightful perspectives on how some dad's experience fatherhood.

Candid Questions & Answers from Men about Fatherhood

Q1. Do you feel like you are a 'present' dad?

Interview Answers
- 30% said 'Yes,' they felt they were present as dads.
- 70% said 'No,' they weren't as present as they wanted to be.

Q2. Do you feel like you are 'available' physically, mentally, and emotionally for your child(ren)? And if not, which area(s) do you feel needs improvement?

Interview Answers
- 20% said that they were present in all three areas.
- 20% said they needed to improve on being available 'mentally.'
- 50% said they needed a great deal of improvement in all areas dealing with 'emotions.'
- 10% said they needed to improve on being available 'physically.'

Q3. What do you 'enjoy' most about being a dad?

Interview Answers
- I love for my children to feel like they can depend on me. I am grateful that they make me accountable. And

I love that they like to learn about what I've learned during my lifetime.

- What I enjoy most is being able to see a creation that came from me – better versions of myself! I love seeing some of my characteristics in them and how they manifest in so many ways. And because they were raised differently from me, I can still see their innocence. To see them experience life before things try to creep in and tarnish their views and feelings – has been special.

- Unfortunately, I was not as present when my children were growing up. My career required a lot of travel. And when I was at home during the weekends, I prioritized my performances with my band because we had gigs on most weekends. This also meant that I didn't spend a lot of quality time with my children, which I do regret. However, I am grateful to have the opportunity to watch my daughter be a mother to my grandchildren. She is a TERRIFIC mom and has done a great job developing a strong bond with her children. And this really makes me happy to see!

- I enjoy EVERYTHING about being a dad. As a student and leader of the Bible, I genuinely enjoy seeing and experiencing the correlation between how God parents us and how he provides a blueprint for us to use as well.

- Being 70 years old, I can say that I've been afforded a great opportunity to watch my daughter grow into a wonderful young woman with a husband and son of her own. Being able to witness her growth in the midst of experiencing the challenges she faced during the split between her mom and me has been encouraging. I realize that having her go back and forth between her mom and me – was tough. So, seeing her push through all of the issues that came with the challenges between her mom and me, and the other unnecessary trauma and chaos she experienced with her mom – showed me how strong she was. Seeing her grow into such a strong, beautiful, and brilliant woman has been an inspiring sight to see!

In addition to witnessing her maturity, I also have the privilege of sharing a common faith with her. And to see that the fruits I invested in faith actually turned into her having her own relationship with the Lord is one of the greatest blessings I've experienced as her dad!

I only have one stepdaughter, and I came into her life when she was an infant, and I was 17 years old. There were many things that I can recall enjoying early on, but now that she's 24 years old and has matured, I can really appreciate being a part of her entire growth experience!

I am also very happy that I had enough sense to make the choice to be there for her and her mother as a 17-year-old boy because it helped me become the man that I am.

Fatherhood has given me the opportunity to nurture the soul of another, which is the absolute greatest gift I've ever received!

Q4. What do you find to be most 'challenging' about being a dad?

Interview Answers

- Trying to do everything right so that I can be a 'good' example for my kids. It's challenging because you can never REALLY be sure if you're being a good and attentive parent. You never truly know if what you're doing as a parent is the 'right' thing to do, which is a challenge for me because I like to know how I'm doing right away. So, waiting to see if the lessons I taught were beneficial or totally off base makes me uneasy at times.

- The most challenging aspect of parenting for me right now is dealing with the fact that I am raising my four kids alone. The choices and actions that I made during my relationship with my kids' mother resulted in our separation. So, dealing with "what ifs" hasn't been easy. And it was extremely challenging to make the decision to step up as the primary parent of my four kids. I've raised my children as a single father for most of their lives now, and not too long ago, a couple of my oldest wanted to spend more time with their mom and decided to move in with her. I can't lie; that was very challenging to process, but I'm happy I rolled with it, as everything is working out.

- Making emotional connections, especially with my daughters, has been tough! Demonstrating patience is also a challenge for me, and this is true for both my son and daughters. I'm in counseling now, as I realize that my lack of patience goes a little deeper than anything that my kids are doing or not doing. With my wife's help, I realized I needed to do some 'inside' work – so I decided to put in the work and see how it goes.

■ Raising children as young Christian parents was incredibly challenging. Trying to strike the right balance between doing what we 'thought' our kids needed versus what they 'really' needed was hard. My wife and I struggled with trying to reinforce biblical principles and values with our kids in a practical way while trying to keep in mind that the world they were growing up in was vastly different from what we were used to.

To be completely transparent, I don't feel like I did a very good job as a father with my first couple of kids. But thank the Lord, I got the opportunity to make the necessary corrections as we had each kid, so I got better and better. I'm also happy that my mistakes didn't completely ruin the relationships with my kids. After having five kids, I felt like we finally got the whole 'parenting' process down!

One other area that I found exceedingly difficult for me at times was dealing with the 'emotional' side of things. I'm innately a direct person, and I felt like 'emotions' were unclear, so I had to be very patient and deliberate about how I responded to situations that were emotionally driven. But I also learned that when the approach I was used to didn't work, I figured

I'd better try something different. I never wanted my response to result in consequences that would damage my kids, so I really worked on how to get out of my own way so that I could become what they needed.

- It's really challenging for me to say 'no' to my children. I want them to always feel like they can come to me about anything! So, when I say 'no,' I feel like it will eventually result in them not wanting to come to me for help. And I don't like the idea of them not coming to me.

- I've been told that I struggle with allowing my daughter and her husband to find their own way – and I would have to agree! It's hard to allow them to jump over certain hurdles if I can help them. I realize that it is a current fact that even though my baby girl and son are well into their 40s with their own kids, I'm still working on allowing them to use their wings to fly. I'm sure that I'm doing a little better and will continue to make progress!

- One of the biggest challenges I have, like so many other dads I know, is that I sometimes lose sight of the 'big picture.' I can sometimes get caught up in executing a particular task or taking care of priorities that I forget how important it is to provide my kids with undivided attention. I'm learning that all of these 'small' moments are just as important as the 'big' moments. So, I'm really working to make sure that my daughter knows that I'm fully present because I value spending time with her. All the moments we spend together are equally special to me.

Q5. Does anything about fatherhood scare you? If so, what?

Interview Answers

- Having all young black sons and dealing with the current realities in our world, it's hard for me not to feel like they are targets. I feel like my sons, as well as other black boys/young men, are being 'actively' pursued and sabotaged — and this is my #1 fear. Like many other parents, I don't want my kids in trouble at all, but I especially do not want them to get caught up in any negative interactions with the legal system, whether it is because of their actions, the people they're with, or just being in the wrong place at the wrong time. I know the system personally. I know that once a kid is in the system, it can be very challenging for them to truly break free. It's like once you're in the system, you may get 'extended' chains, so you don't have to remain locked up, but you remain connected in more ways than anyone can truly explain. So, I'm doing whatever I can to help my sons make better decisions and explore paths that have legitimate opportunities.
- I want my kids to be proud of me! I NEVER want to be an embarrassment to them or for them to be ashamed of me. Their view of me is a BIG DEAL and of HIGH importance to me. I believe they know this! However, I still have concerns about my ability to be everything

they need me to be as a father. I know that I'm human and flawed, but I would never want my flaws to change the way that my children look at me or interact with me. So, not being what my kids need when they need it scares me.

- My limitations make me very uncomfortable when I'm unable to be all things, do all things, or be everywhere my kids need me. This limitation scares me because I can't and don't want to imagine not being present to help them when they need me most.

- EVERYTHING scares me when it comes to raising my kids in the world today, especially my boys. As a black man who was caught up in the legal system myself for a while, I know how the system works, and I don't want my sons to ever get caught up in it.

- Getting this parenting role all wrong and having to deal with the MESS I created – scares the HECK out of me. But I've come to the conclusion that we will MESS up (A LOT) – so I must simply be prepared to take ownership, be willing to address any messy areas that I helped to create and be okay with growing from it.

- After 69 years on my journey, I would say that there is not much that scares me. I trust God so much with my life and my children that I believe He will always equip us with what is necessary to address whatever comes our way.

- So many things about fatherhood scare me! Parenting is truly a role that requires you to fly blind! There are no instructional manuals that come with your specific child, and even if you've already had some experience, there's no guarantee how much of your experience can be used with the various children you may have.

- The other thing that scares me is the whole cause-and-effect dynamic. The time it takes for the 'impact' of certain 'actions/experiences' that our children have or witnessed is not always noticeable. Our kids can have challenging or traumatic experiences with other people or us throughout life that they may not know how to verbalize or might be scared to - and this scares me BIG TIME! To think that my kids could be struggling with something on their own, especially if I could protect or help them in any way, terrifies me.

- Having limited control over all things that involve or impact my kids. Seeing all the outside influences that are constantly and aggressively competing for my kid's attention makes my nerves HELLA bad! And given the fact that I don't have primary or even shared custody of my boys at this time makes me feel like I have limited opportunities to really make the impacts that I want to make, and I don't like the shit one bit!

Q6. Do you have any 'relationship' goals for you and your kids?

Interview Answers

- Yes, for my youngest son, my goal is to keep our relationship going and growing. I think our relationship is right on track, and our bond is strong.

    For my older boys, my goal is to form a stronger bond with them. I want it to become relaxed, as I feel like there are moments of discomfort and tension due to the approach I used when I was raising them, but we never actually talk about it. Like we always say, hindsight is 20/20; I can now see that I was too hard on them sometimes. I often pushed them to do what I wanted without asking or considering their thoughts and feelings. Unfortunately, I believe that this has created the awkward and uncomfortable moments we experience. To be honest, I don't even know if my sons even feel the way I feel about the mistakes I believe I made. Who knows, I may be the only one thinking about these moments, and I also may be the one creating the awkwardness because of my regret. Since I feel like my relationship is good overall with my older boys, it's hard for me to initiate conversations about certain topics that I believe might change. However, my goal is to push myself to start having conversations with my older sons about their upbringing to see if the thoughts and stories that I've told myself all these years are valid.

Yes, but I have different goals for my sons versus my daughter. When it comes to my sons, I want to be a good example for them. I want to show them the character of a man and how to treat women. I always want them to feel comfortable coming to me to talk about ANY topic, especially when they need advice.

When it comes to my daughter, I want her to know that I will ALWAYS be there to cover her with my life – NO MATTER what the situation is!

Yes, my primary goal is to be a positive and productive example for them (my sons and daughter). It's important to me to cultivate and maintain relationships that will allow me to continue to help them become mature and independent in their thoughts and actions.

I desire to have 'individual' and 'unique' bonds with all my children because it gives me insight into who they are as individuals. My number one goal in our relationship is to help them make new connections, experiences, and new revelations. I believe that I can accomplish this goal if I make knowing them on a 'personal' level a top priority.

Yes, my primary goal is for my children to always know that they are a priority to me, and that I will always SHOW UP for all four of them!

I honestly desire a relationship with my grown children that allows us to stay in constant communication. I know that they have their own lives, but I want to be part of it. My primary relationship goal is for my children and me to stay CONNECTED!

▣ My only goal is to effectively pass down a legacy that provides my children with a solid foundation to build on.

Establishing and maintaining meaningful relationships are EXTREMELY important to my wife and me, so providing insight that we've learned over our 50 years of marriage is important to include in the legacy we pass down.

▣ I always want my daughter to know that I am on her team – now and always!

Q7. Did you grow up with a dad who was 'present' and 'available'?

Interview Answers

▣ 20% said 'Yes,' their dads were present and available to them as they were growing up.

▣ 80% said 'No,' their dads were one of the following:
   • Unknown
   • Not 'physically' present
   • 'Physically' present but unavailable/disengaged in all other areas

Q8. How do you feel your relationship or lack of relationship with your dad has impacted your approach to fatherhood?

Interview Answers

▣ My father was VERY hands-on! My mother died when I was 11 years old, and my dad was determined to give me what he felt I needed to grow. In addition to being a 'single dad,' he was a coach to me in all areas of life. He played NO GAMES with me, especially when it came to learning about the 'quality' and 'character' of a man. I'm not saying that I always received the lessons, nor was I always open to what he was trying to teach me. What I'm saying is that he was committed to making sure he did his part and would put me in check REAL QUICK if I was struggling to level up! His consistent presence and active engagement taught me that life will dish out some major blows, but it didn't relieve me of my responsibilities to be a FULL-TIME father to my children. He taught me through his words and actions that there is never a valid reason for me not to be present for my kids. I learned that not only did I need to be present, but I needed to be actively pursuing a growing relationship with them. My dad set a 'blueprint' for me, and I'm determined to follow it as best as I can!

▪ Although my dad was around, I did not feel like he was present or available. So, I promised myself that I would be a better father than he was. I was determined to be the opposite of him, so I invested a lot of my time focusing on ways to create a better experience for my children. What I learned is that if your focus isn't balanced, you can also create unhealthy relationships unintentionally.

▪ Having a relationship with my dad, even though I lived with my mom in another city, was beyond essential to my life. I would say without hesitation that my dad's presence in my life - SAVED MY LIFE!

My dad gave me a family structure. He instilled a high importance of family into all of his kids, even though we didn't have the same moms. He sacrificed EVERYTHING for his kids and had to encounter a lot of bullshit to stay connected to us, but it never stopped him.

I never got to meet my real dad, but my stepdad came into my life when I was 10, and he was AMAZING! I would say that my stepdad's presence and actions provided me with a good example of what a father should be, which has helped me immensely.

The relationship I have with my dad impacted every aspect of how I approached fatherhood. My dad was and still is a PHENOMENAL man and father! I truly tried to model his approach to fatherhood with my children. I thought I was doing a wonderful job trying to implement the same fatherhood 'formula' my dad used to raise me. But what I learned was that the 'formula' approach doesn't work!

I learned that fatherhood does not have a 'one size' fits all formula. Not only are our kids uniquely designed, but there are also so many other variables like the culture, region you live in, and family dynamics that play a major role in the process. There are so many other unpredictable things that impact and influence how we raise our children that were not around when my dad raised me. So, I quickly learned that taking the 'formula-based' approach to parenting wasn't the most effective approach, even if I felt like my dad's approach was the BEST. His approach with me was what was best for me!

Unfortunately, I didn't know my biological dad until I was 13. But fortunately, I had a stepdad who was one AMAZING man! Throughout my life, I could always tell that my stepdad was invested in me — even when I didn't understand why he would want to be.

He introduced me to church and was a great example of how faith was actually walked out in 'real' life. Initially, I didn't buy-in to the whole 'faith' thing until I was 18. Now, as a 48-year-old man, I can wholeheartedly tell you that I am so glad that everything clicked when I was 18 because I can't IMAGINE what my life and my family would have been like without a relationship with the Lord.

Although my father was physically present and mentally engaging, he was also emotionally disconnected. When it came to displaying or addressing anything that included emotions, he was and still is distant and emotionally unavailable!

His emotional distance taught me that I had a responsibility to establish a 'healthy' emotional foundation. A foundation that emphasized the importance of acknowledging and addressing emotions. And I must say that I am proud of my progress and how my determination to initiate discussions about feelings/ emotions truly has paid off. I feel like my daughter and I can talk about ANYTHING, and she knows that her feelings matter to me! She also knows that I won't make it awkward or uncomfortable when she's on an emotional rollercoaster. I'm happy to say that my approach is working!

◾ My father was not present at all. And what's interesting about this is that his father wasn't present for him when he was growing up, and he disowned him. I use the word interesting because it baffles me anytime I think about how a person can intimately know the pain and struggle of not having their father present and still perpetuate the cycle. Not because it was hard to access me or because my mom caused him issues, but simply because he decided to be somewhere else.

Needless to say, this destructive cycle stops with me. My sons will NEVER experience this! My sons will know me as I am – and I will always be intentionally present, available, and active in every aspect of their lives!

Q9. What are 'lessons learned' or 'best practices' that you would share with other men about fatherhood?

Interview Answers

◾ Take time to assess your approach to fatherhood and do whatever you need to do to adjust whenever needed.

◾ Avoid being overbearing simply because you are the 'authority' figure. Take the time to explore your kids' thoughts and be deliberate about supporting them - it helps to build their confidence.

- Instead of always doing what you want your kids to or pushing your personal agenda – especially when it comes to sports or any area that you may want your kids to explore – stop and ask them what their interests/thoughts are!

- Kids are ALWAYS watching us – and they imitate what they see, not what we say.

- Show up, be consistent, and create accountability! Sometimes we (dads) may be tempted not to follow through on something because we don't have our SHIT together – so we duck and dodge, not thinking about how we appear to be inconsistent to our kids. But we really need to cut all that out and just SHOW UP ANYWAY! SHOW UP, even if you don't have the money to run the kids around town to buy all types of shit. Most of the time, it doesn't even matter as much as we think it does. SHOW UP even if the mother of your kids is trippin' – you ain't there to see her no way! SHOW UP if we mess up – keep it real, acknowledge your mistake, and apologize. Then, work hard to stop bull-shittin' because the bottom line is that our kids just want us to SHOW UP to see them and hear about what makes them happy or sad. They just want us to be into them! They want us to be their biggest and most dependable fan and supporter!

- Build a support system throughout your community so that your kids know that people are paying attention to how they behave when you're not around. A support system that you and your kids can trust and respect so that when your kids may have to be 'checked,' there won't be any problems with the correction that was extended.

- Say "sorry" when you're wrong – and mean it! Our kids already know what the deal is, and most of the time, they're just waiting to see how we'll actually hold ourselves accountable. Show them that it's ok to acknowledge and own your mistakes at any age.

- Continue to Learn! We (parents) need to continue to learn about all things, especially when it comes to having business savvy. We need to invest our time, money, and attention into reading 'good' books so that we can teach our kids – and encourage them to do the same.

- Don't try to mold your kids into a version of you! Our kids don't need to become us; they should be who they were designed to be. Our job is simply to provide them with exposure, support, and sometimes other resources that will help them thrive!

- As your children grow older, work to transition from an 'instructor/director' parent role to an 'influencer/supporter' role. Be willing to be flexible and intentional, especially when their 'lifestyle' does not meet your expectations and may not be comfortable or convenient for you.

- Always remember that we cannot make our kids who we are or want them to be. So, be careful of what demands you place on them. If you're not careful, everything can backfire on you. If this happens, your kids may resent and reject the very lessons they need to grow and excel in life.

- Be careful about navigating your relationships as a man, spouse, dad, and friend because our kids watch what we do.
- If you invest the time to create a child – then you need to be just as invested in taking care of the child you helped to create!
- This is a little different, but I do think that we (men) could and should hold each other more accountable, especially when we know that we're not doing our part as fathers, spouses, etc. I can recall meeting up with my boys many times at a bar or local spot to watch a game or just decompress - knowing that one of the homies had no business hanging with us. Whether it was because he spent more time and cash flow with us than he contributed to taking care of his situations or that he was completely lost in the areas of fatherhood or relationship management, knowing too much made us HELLA uncomfortable. So, none of us would say much of anything to address the matter at hand. And if we did say something, it would be really brief – perhaps asking if everything was good at home, with the kids, family, etc. If his response was anything close to "I'm straight" or "I'm good," then that was the end of that. I know it sounds bad, but it's true!

I'm sure we responded this way for various reasons. Some of us may not have spoken up because we had our own issues at home and didn't feel like we could correct someone else without being called out on our stuff! Others may have felt like our guy needed a space to relax and clear his mind and didn't want to take that moment away because men rarely get to decompress 'fully.'

So, my recommendation is that we (men) should make it a common practice to be more vocal about areas we know need to be addressed instead of taking the approach of 'let me mind my business.' Hell, we (men) all need to start talking more anyway and holding each other accountable more, especially when it comes to being present for our kids / family.

- If you don't have the best relationships with individuals who are 'primary' caretakers or influencers (i.e., babies-moms, grandparents.) in your child(ren) lives, do whatever you can to figure out how to better manage those relationships. Life is so much better for EVERYONE when the relationships are flowing smoothly!

- Stay away from 'formula-based' parenting, aka "If I follow these steps, I'll be the perfect parent for my child." – TRUST ME, it doesn't work! Take the time to learn and grow with your children because they're all different. They're all dealing with different variables in life, some things you may be familiar with and others that will be new to you. Taking the 'personalized' approach will create unique and special bonds that will last a lifetime and beyond!

■ Live more authentically! Our kids need to see that we are human. Humans who are flawed and in need of grace and forgiveness. We are humans willing to do what is necessary to learn and grow even as we age. If we fail to live life with an appropriate level of transparency, our children can become confused and struggle with differentiating what a 'facade is' and what is 'real,' which will not benefit them as they journey through life.

■ Fight for your family...your kids...your spouse/significant others...and all-important relationships! Don't be so quick or willing to give up, especially when your situations aren't easy to manage. We must do better at pushing through things!

■ Pray for your children by name daily – and be specific with the blessing you pray over their lives!

■ It's never too late to try to correct your mistake! Everything will work out in time if you can be genuine, open, and willing to pursue and extend forgiveness. But know that you may not be able to recover all aspects of the relationship – which is okay. Be careful to appreciate the progress you can make and take it one day... one encounter at a time!

■ Maximize the time you have with your children NOW! Be careful not to operate under the notion that you'll have time later – because later is not promised to you nor to your children. Not only because you or your kid(s) might pass away, but your kids may 'choose' not to invest the time just like you decided not to at some point. Cycles can be vicious, and when they are unhealthy, they don't do anyone any good. So, we must work to be more intentional and wiser!

- Take the time to listen to your kids. As adults, at times, we don't take time to understand what our children need from us on a spiritual, mental, and emotional level. Unfortunately, our lack of attentiveness can also lead to our kids being dismissive of our opinions and advice. It might also lead them to seek and/or prefer the thoughts and guidance from others, which can be dangerous if they don't have your child(ren)'s best interest in mind.

- DO NOT be afraid or hold back from correcting and disciplining your kids. Since I always wanted to stay connected with my kids, I was hesitant to tell them 'no' out of fear that they would not include me in their decision process. TRUST me, as they get older, others will correct them. If we fail to help them figure out how to work through tough times, our children will have challenges as they grow and journey in REAL life. Our responsibility is to prepare and equip our kids to develop good relationships.

- Take the time to share important 'growth/maturity' moments with your kids. For example, tell them about times when you failed to make the right decisions, what you felt like, how it impacted you, and how you recovered. And if you didn't get the opportunity to recover – tell them how that made you feel. Sharing our experiences – the good, bad, and ugly – with transparency really helps our kids learn in ways that cannot always be explained.

- Do your best to REALLY hear your kids out. It REALLY helps you learn A LOT!
- Appreciate your gifts. Be sure to treat your kids and fatherhood as gifts. Having this mindset helps us remember that not everyone has the opportunity to be in their kid's lives. Be willing to sacrifice - When we decide to have kids, we should already know that it will require sacrifice. Be willing to do what it takes to make sure our sacrifices have positive results.
- Demonstrate unconditional love. There is something POWERFUL and LIFE CHANGING about extending and receiving 'unconditional love.' Do your best to be the first person your children experience this with. You want them to know how it feels to be loved with all of their flaws and quirkiness. You also want them to know how it feels to be encouraged and challenged to grow past their comfort zones.
- Do whatever you can to give your children a good foundation – a foundation of spiritual, faith awareness, grace, truthfulness, love, and patience…for themselves and others!
- Consistent quality time with your kids is a MUST! Do not allow yourself or your kids to become so caught up in life that you become distant.
- Keep it REAL without involving your kids in all the 'adult' details. Often, the picture painted about dads is not the best. We (dads) must work to find the right

balance of correcting the perception/narratives without getting caught up in the distractions that are SURE to come our way – especially when we're trying to do right! I share this because sometimes we (dads and moms) give our kids way too much info at the wrong times (typically when we're emotional or focused on our own agenda). When we do this, we run the risk of putting them in the middle of adult drama. However, if we don't inform them enough or we (dads) are not 'present' to balance out the story, we run the risk of our kids having a 'one-sided' skewed narrative that could take years for us to help clarify and resolve.

- Don't allow 'little' issues to override the 'big picture.' The 'big picture' is all about developing a strong relationship with your children. So, we (men) must do whatever we can to keep the 'main thing' the 'MAIN THING!' AVOID any and all distractions as much as we can!

- Be sure to invest in the emotional growth and maturity of your children. Don't be afraid to seek out help if you don't know how to support them.

- Pay close attention to the amount of time you really have with your children – and ask yourself what you would like to do with the time you have left with them.

- Provide your children with undivided attention so you can really get to know who they are. Our kids have their own personalities, and sometimes, we must learn to adjust accordingly. It's also important to remember that adjusting how we engage with our children doesn't diminish our authority. However, it does have the power to help us grow and improve our relationships.

▪ Seek out ways where you can offer your presence, support, and / or resources that might be helpful to your children. BUT remember to not get in your feelings if they decide not to consider or receive your offers or support right away.

▪ Be honest and transparent – kids respect authenticity.

Q10. Do you feel that the mother of your child(ren) can influence/impact the way you approach fatherhood? If so, please share ways women can 'HELP' or 'HINDER' you as a dad.

Interview Answers: Ways Women Can HELP

▪ Women help us a LOT when they genuinely extend opportunities to partner with us to do what is in the best interest of our children, especially if we are no longer together. If we're not doing our part, instead of withholding our child(ren) from us, perhaps try a different method, like suggesting time with a mediator or someone who can provide balanced guidance and keep us focused on the kids. I realize that some of us men are not open to this approach, but some of us are, so it's worth a try. Another approach that I know can help is if women take the time to write us a note to share what they feel are disconnects or issues that are resulting in something counterproductive for our child(ren). Of course, it would help if it's specific, concise, and respectful.

- It helps when women take the time to learn about what encourages us as fathers and men. It also helps when we're allowed to be who we are (as men and fathers) and learn along the way – just like women/mothers have to.
- It's helpful when women work with us in a respectful way to establish roles, responsibilities, and boundaries. We sometimes recognize that when there's no discussion around these topics, we tend to overstep. My point is that 'mature' discussions are always helpful. And BOTH parties must be willing to engage to ensure the best thing is done for our kids.
- Women can be such good listeners, especially when they are helping to bridge the gap between dads and their kids. As men, we often struggle with making the emotional connections needed to 'REALLY' address the heart of certain matters.

  I'm very grateful that my wife listens and then gives me the feedback that I 'NEED' to hear in a way that she knows will reach me.
- I believe that there is something powerful about a woman/mother who takes the time to build men/fathers up through prayer and verbal affirmations!
- The way women approach conversations can be extremely helpful, especially when she has insight on a topic or area that I cannot see. I typically find that when dealing with the 'emotional' side of things where

I need to think about various aspects, my wife helps me out a ton.

- There are no words to describe how helpful it is when the mother of my children takes the time to understand where I'm coming from.
- When a mother demonstrates a willingness to partner with consideration and cooperation when situations are not ideal.
- Seeing how invested my wife is in her role as a mother is truly inspiring! Not only is she invested in her role as a biological mother to our two girls, but she's also an AMAZING bonus mom to my son! Watching her truly inspires me to be a better father!
- When my wife asks me questions in a manner that helps me think and then plants a few things I can do to address or correct a situation – it helps me every time! She knows how to share her recommendation directly, but not aggressively – and it typically sticks with me! I learned a lot about how to approach conversations with my kids by copying my wife! Her style seems to work, so why not use it?
- When mothers are supportive of fathers who are working to guide their sons – and they demonstrate their support by giving them the space they need to work through things!
- Be mindful that we both have roles – I'm the dad, and you are the mom. My role does not take away from yours – it's just different. Our roles are supposed to complement each other.

Interview Answer: Ways Women Can HINDER

- When women make dads feel like their presence in the life of their child(ren) does not matter. When a father feels like his presence is 'optional' and not a 'necessity,' it can begin to impact how much value he feels he brings to his child(ren) or the family unit.
- It is hurtful, toxic, and traumatizing when mothers use kids as bait or a weapon to carry out their self-serving agenda. This not only hinders a man's ability to be a present dad, but it is horrible for the overall health and well-being of our child(ren).
- It's EXTREMELY important that women become more attentive to the 'masculine' energy that they put off. Especially for women that have been exposed to having to hold all things down without a man present (i.e., exposure either through her upbringing or her personal experiences as an adult).
- When mothers imply that a dad's perspective or feelings on a topic are unimportant, it's also challenging to co-parent with a person who speaks to us in an emasculating or condescending way. Her communication style and delivery can also be hindering, especially if she doesn't share critical information that we should know about our child(ren) – either because she doesn't feel like we need to know or she's withholding it to hurt us.
- There is something that happens to a man's ego when his actions as a 'father,' 'husband,' or 'man' are corrected in front of his kids (young or old). To all mothers

and women, PLEASE...PLEASE...PLEASE use more discretion when you need to provide (dads) with corrective feedback, especially if you want us to truly hear and process what you've shared. I'm sure that 99.9% of the time, we NEED to hear what you have to share with us, but delivery, timing, and environment are EXTREMELY important.

■ When moms either disrespect dads in front of the kids or say negative remarks about us when we're not around.

■ When moms assume that the actions we take are about them versus our kids. Like if we (dads) demonstrate a level of care and concern about her well-being simply because you want to make sure that she's good when our kids are with her – and then it's assumed that we still want her. Now, I will say that lines can get blurred in some situations. However, when we have made an agreement about how we will co-parent, it shouldn't be randomly changed if our (the parents') relationship is in flux, especially if it has to do with dating. It is also extremely important to discuss how both parties will navigate in other relationships and how involved the kids will be during the co-parenting discussions.

■ When moms compare us (dads) to other men in their lives in an 'unhealthy' manner – especially if the man the mom is comparing the dad to is a piece of shit that doesn't take care of his responsibilities. When the mom praises another man like he's the 'man' or 'father' of the year, simply because he is catering to all of her needs. It doesn't matter whether he is a 'deadbeat' to his own kids or a bum that doesn't work. We can't forget about the men that have an abundance of cash but don't take care of their own kid(s) and would prefer to use it to floss or fulfill their own desires. When a dad has to encounter all of this foolishness, when he's simply trying to form a 'personal' relationship with his child – it can become overwhelming.

■ Mothers that REALLY believe that they can operate as the 'mother and father.' This way of thinking is divisive and harmful on many levels – and it can hinder the relationship dynamics between children and their fathers. It's clear that some dads have abandoned their position– leaving mothers to do more than they should have to do. However, we still cannot support the idea that fathers / men can be replaced by mothers / women. It is so important that our kids understand how to cultivate relationships with dads / men and moms / women. We must teach them that neither can be replaced by the opposite and that both are needed. However, when a father refuses to level up, I would encourage mothers to seek out a 'trusted' male role model or support crew if possible.

■ We have MAJOR issues when dads encounter women operating in their 'pseudo' masculine energy – and believe that they can provide a 'father-like' experience to children. Anytime a woman uses what feels like an attempt to take on the 'father' role, you can guarantee that there is going to be a clash.

■ The 'smoke and mirror' kind of moms are extremely problematic on too many levels to adequately explain. It is unfortunate when mothers are 'automatically' assumed to be the most 'suitable' parent simply because she is the 'mom' when this may not be the case. Far too often, it is assumed that mothers will make the physical, mental, and emotional well-being of their children a priority, which is presumptuously dangerous! Unfortunately, there are some mothers who are also extremely careless and self-absorbed – and the well-being of their child(ren) is the last thing on their minds. Please don't get me wrong, there are a TON of amazing mothers doing their thing, but there are some that are 'disconnected' emotionally and mentally – and they just have the kids physically. Again, this can be a MAJOR problem because when you have a dad who is taking care of his business to be 'actively present,' his efforts can be sabotaged by a mother that may be 'disconnected' and 'divisive.'

■ Stop being overprotective or 'babying' young men – it's really not healthy for their maturity, independence, or confidence. Raising overly 'dependent' kids is never good, but when our young men are not conditioned to walk confidently with independent thoughts and actions, it can be crippling to generations.

Q11. Finish this statement: "When my child(ren) speaks of me, I want them to say that I am a _____ dad."

Interview Responses:

Below are the attributes/characteristics dads desired the most:

Approachable, Attentive, Available, Caring, Compassionate, Encouraging, Fun, Hardworking, Humble, Generous, Giving, God-fearing, Influential, Knowledgeable, Loving, Nice, Supportive, Present, Reliable, and Responsible.

Mid-Interview 'Call to Action'

After the dads provided the attributes they wanted their child(ren) to use when describing them, I challenged them to do one simple thing. I asked them to go and ask their child(ren) what words they would use to describe them as fathers. I asked them to use an approach that would make their young and/or adult child(ren) feel safe and comfortable sharing their authentic feelings. I also asked them to hold back on providing any responses and to watch their body language. The mission of the 'mid-interview call to action' was for the dads to invest time to learn more about their child(ren)'s actual experience instead of the narratives they validated on their own. I reminded them that our children view us through different lenses and vantage points – where our intentions have little influence, especially if they have not created impactful or positive realities.

> *"**Missions** are always jeopardized when we do not take the time to acquire understanding from different vantage points."*
>
> *— Unknown*

Once the fathers accomplished the mission of obtaining insight into how their children viewed their character and role as a dad, they could begin to compare their "perspective" vs. "reality." This was an important action step because some of the dads thought they had failed significantly with some of their kids and thought that their children would not have any positive words to share about them, which was not true. This helped the dads remember that validating the narratives we tell ourselves is also important because we can sometimes be our worst critics and/or have a skewed perspective.

This exercise also helped to reinforce the power of communication and the importance of seeking understanding. It revealed how the counterproductive narratives we have in our minds can damage our ability to develop connections with those we love most. This exercise reminded them that we (humans) could recall things in an unbalanced way – either we are terribly hard on ourselves, or we avoid accountability, which damages us and others.

Again, the key objective of this 'call to action' exercise was to learn more about 'perceptions' vs. 'reality.' The best way to summarize this is by looking at it from an 'If...Then' perspective.

If...	Then...
If the dad's descriptions about himself as a father were more *positive* than his child's/children's reality...	Then the exercise served as lessons learned that would help the dad discover areas he needed to work on to ensure his child(ren) could experience him in the positive way described.
If the dad's descriptions about himself as a father were more *critical* than his child's/children's reality ...	Then the exercise created an opportunity that could help release the dad from some counterproductive narratives/thoughts by learning the words/attributes to describe their 'actual' experience.

This 'call to action' exercise was simple yet extremely powerful. I encourage all parents (dads and moms) to try it. We are never too old to learn about ourselves, especially if it helps us build stronger relationships and connections.

Q12. Do you view God as a Father figure?

Interview Answers

- 15% said 'Yes,' they viewed God as a Father figure.
- 85% said 'No,' they did not view God as a Father figure.

Below are some perspectives shared about this question:

Interview Answers

- Yes, I've always viewed God as a father to me. I believe He is and has always been the one helping me to provide for my family. I speak to Him through prayer, and I also say confessions to express my trust. He has been faithful in protecting and providing for my family, even in some of my toughest and weakest moments. I believe that is exactly what a good father does for his children.

- Yes, I pray daily, give thanks, and then follow up with a request for wisdom and guidance to help me be a better father.

- Not really, although I am Catholic, and I acknowledge God in a spiritual aspect. However, I do not view him as a 'father figure.' Having a 'physical' connection is huge for me in a relationship, so viewing him as a 'father' is hard for me to see.

- Yes, God has proven to me that He can do something in a man's heart that is unlike the human father. The way He constantly extends compassion and love for me, blows my mind!

To be honest, I never really thought about God in the role of a 'father,' but now that we're talking about it – I believe that is what Jesus was implying when He was teaching the disciples to pray! (LOL). Wait a min – I do remember the Lord's prayer when Jesus was teaching the disciples to pray. He did say, "Our Father which art in Heaven..." (WOW)!

Shay, go ahead and put my response as "YES!" I will now view God in a new way – as a Father, which is a way I never thought of before!

No, I don't. Perhaps it's because my father wasn't around, and I correlate with a father in a physical sense. I can't imagine making a 'father'-like connection in a non-physical way, but it's something for me to think more about.

Yes, there's NO WAY that I could be living the life that I live – and doing the things that I do still at 69 years old without recognizing God as my 'Lord, Savior, and Father!'

He demonstrates His fatherly presence to me by extending me His unconditional love, undeserved grace, continuous forgiveness, unlimited protection, constant presence, endless provision, and in so many other ways. You can probably tell that I can keep going, but I'll stop here (LOL).

My desire is to be an 'earthly' image of what He is to me for my children — and I am determined to keep working at it throughout my days on this earth!

When the Lord instructed me to conclude my interview questions by asking the dads, "If they viewed Him as a Father figure?" - I had a lot of questions (which the Lord is used to with me...LOL). One of my main questions was why He wanted it to be the last question. Why didn't He want it to be closer to the questions about their experience with their earthly fathers? What He shared with me was that He wanted the last question to give them something to ponder – as His desire is that all men and women experience Him as their Father in a more intimate way.

I'm not sure that many men/dads truly understand how much the Lord desires a 'close' and 'active' relationship with them. What I found to be interesting is the same way that the dads expressed their desire and need to have close and engaging relationships with their children – aligned with the relationship God desires to have with them. I'm also not sure that many of us realize one of the primary names that God chooses to be addressed as is 'Abba' (Aramaic for Father). There are so many scriptures and promises that include the father/child relationship. Here are a couple of my favorites that I encourage you to ponder:

Psalm 68:5- "A Father to the Fatherless..."

This reminds me that the creator of all things extended an offer to those like me (and some of you) who may not know who their biological father is or do not have a relationship with him.

2 Corinthians 6:18-
"...and I will be a Father to you, and you shall be sons and
daughters to me, says the Lord Almighty."

I love this because it reminds us of how the Lord views us.

My point is this: I believe that the Lord has something extremely special that is reserved for His children. However, we can only experience this when we accept Him as our "Abba" Father.

Post-Interview Thoughts

Again, hearing these dads speak with such vulnerability about how they desired to be seen and known by their children was unlike any other experience I've had! It reminded me that what is seen with the eyes or heard by the ears doesn't always provide an adequate or accurate picture. It reminded me how important basic communication and listening skills are to developing, building, and preserving ALL relationships, especially if we value them! It also reminded me that most people are willing to share their stories and the issues they're still dealing with when they feel safe to do so and they feel like it will serve a purpose. It confirmed that we must begin the work on initiating, engaging, and supporting continued conversations about this topic. We must begin to properly nourish relationships between dads and their children... as well as the co-parent partnership.

There's no doubt that we have a LOT of work to do — but there's also NO DOUBT that we have everything we need to get the work done! So, don't stop here; keep reading because the chapters ahead will provide you with some practical insight that you can adopt and apply immediately.

CHAPTER 4

Insight from a Grateful I.D. (Intentional Dad) Beneficiary

"Gratitude is the ability to experience the joy of life no matter what! It is an intentional choice that we are empowered to make daily that liberates, encourages, and elevates us in ways that go beyond human comprehension."

– Fa'Shay Halley

Grateful (Adjective)

- Appreciative of benefits received
- Expressing gratitude

Beneficiary (Noun)

"A person (or thing) that receives help or an advantage from something."

99

I titled this chapter 'Insight from a Grateful I.D. (Intentional Dad) Beneficiary' because, by definition, it perfectly describes me. As I shared in Chapter 1, I was fortunate to receive help and advantages throughout my life that came directly from having 'active' relationships with my Heavenly Pops and bonus dads. So, in this chapter, I would like to share more insight into the special relationships that blessed my life.

I also dedicated an entire section within this chapter to highlight some of my favorite 'daddy-daughter' lessons. So, I encourage both dads and moms to check this section out because I believe there are some timeless and precious gems included that can be of great value to any daughter (both young and old).

My Father, a.k.a My Heavenly Pops

Anyone who truly knows me knows that I refer to the Lord as my Heavenly Pops. When I decided to give my life to the Lord in 1996, during my senior year of high school, I had no idea how my relationship with Him would grow to be so intimate. I heard many people speak about having personal relationships with the Lord. But to be honest, I had no idea what they meant. Now, when I think about how much my relationship with the Lord has grown, I truly don't believe anyone could have truly given me adequate insight into what I have experienced. I find it sometimes challenging to find words to fully express my relationship with Him myself. I can say this for certain, I never imagined that I would come to experience Him as my Abba Father. It definitely took me some time to learn about what His offer to be my Father really meant. When I decided to embrace this new relationship dynamic, my heart was enlightened, and my perspective was made new. As I began to experience my relationship with my Heavenly Pops differently, I also started to view some of my life experiences from different vantage points, increasing my level of gratitude. I became more aware of how the Lord had been active and present in my life from the start. It's amazing to see both the full and broken pieces of my journey come together so beautifully – especially through the lenses I see through today!

I believe my Heavenly Pops selected my 'bonus dads' to establish a solid and fruitful foundation to birth a firm sense of faith, confidence, courage, strength, peace, and joy in a girl who was born into a life full of trauma, uncertainty, and dysfunction. Amid the chaos, I was still able to learn how to exchange and embrace grace, love, and respect because of the intentional presence of my Father (Heavenly Pops) and bonus dads.

I want to share a passage that I read recently and would challenge you to take some time alone to read and ponder the insight shared. It is from my new and favorite study Bible titled *"The Tony Evans Study Bible – Christian Standard Bible,"* written by Pastor Tony Evans Sr., and is part of Q&A inserts he has throughout the Bible.

"Question: Jesus told his disciples to pray to God as "Father," emphasizing the relations side of prayer. What would you say to a person who struggles with relating to God as Father?

Answer: A broken relationship or lack of relationship with an earthly father can affect a person's understanding of the heavenly Father. I urge those who've had such experiences not to let a poor earthly father define the heavenly Father. Instead, they should look for other examples. There are good, godly men out there – meant to be emulated, respected, and followed. We should look to those men and, if possible, be mentored by them, not only to see an ongoing illustration of what the heavenly Father is like but to multiply that example by a billion through our own actions!

What you stare at will determine how you feel. You deal with real feelings because of experiences that truly happened to you. So, you need to shift your eyes. Identify a spiritual person who can help you make a clearer connection with your heavenly Father. Then, as you try to increase your intimacy with God, speak to God in his own words. Pray God's Word back to him and assume that what he says is true, even though you may not feel it right now because of your experiences. Again, emulate the right people and assume God is telling the truth. The Holy Spirit's job is to make God's reality real in your life."

Now I realize that everyone may not have the same set of beliefs or desire to read this study bible, which I respect. However, I must stay true to my responsibilities to share insight and resources that I believe can benefit others on their growth journey. I believe the insight highlighted in the quoted text is very beneficial!

As I mentioned, I'm sure several times now, I would never claim that my bonus dads were "perfect." And to be completely transparent, I don't even know much about the spiritual beliefs of a couple of them. But what I do know is that I had a different level of appreciation for each of my bonus dads as I grew closer to my Father in Heaven. It took me some time to get a foundational understanding of what the characteristics of a man, dad, and Father were, but once I did, my life and relationships were never the same.

Once I allowed myself to believe what the Bible said about God being a Father to the fatherless was true, along with the many scriptures that emphasized His character (i.e., as my healer, redeemer, protector, teacher, partner, provider, friend, and more) – my life changed for the better. The more I allowed myself to expand my perspective and embrace the new insight I had, I began to change from the inside out. My change process is still in progress, and I learn something new every day. This means the narrative for my life and my relationships with my Heavenly Father and others must be refreshed daily!

Now, let me address two main questions I've received whenever I share that God is my Heavenly Father:

1. "How can you view God as a father figure when you can't even see him?"
2. "If God is your father and he's always present, then why did he allow you to go through the things you went through?"

And my responses are simple…

- I see, feel, and experience His presence in every aspect of my life daily!

- I don't know why He allows some things to happen, but I know that He has kept His promise to work all things out for my good – converting all my 'messes' into 'lessons and blessings' continues to help me and others in more ways than I have time to share!

- Believing that I was fatherless or would never experience what a 'loving father' was didn't serve me well, so I chose to accept the offer he extended. I pray that you do what's best for you. My goal is not to force what works for me on anyone; I'm simply trying to share lessons learned and best practices. My prayer is that you are open to the insight and pursue what's best for you. As for me, I'm grateful to know Him as my Heavenly Pops.

"She does not stand alone, but with a potent moral force in her life - the love of her Heavenly Father."
- Personalized Quote of Mr. Harper Lee

My Bonus Dads

Now, without any more delays, I am excited to introduce you to my nine bonus dads. I will introduce each of them to you by sharing some of the characteristics I love/loved most about them, along with a 'Special Impact Memory,' which is a story that made a lasting imprint on my life.

Mr. Tommy Sr. – Dad

Tommy had a jovial spirit; he was kind, funny, and super goofy, which is what I loved most about him. And there is no doubt that I am a lot like him in this way, as I am also a HUGE goofball. He would always sing songs randomly and had no problem making songs up (I, too, got this awesome quality - LOL). Our time together was always so special because we could always unapologetically be ourselves.

Special Impact Memory

One day, when I was in the 5th grade, my dad took several buses to come see me at my mom's house. We were both excited when he arrived, and I couldn't wait to give him the new school pictures I had taken. As I went to my room to gather the pictures and write a note on the back, I heard my mom go off on him for who knows what.

For some reason, I had to step away again, and when I came back, my dad was gone, and the pictures I had given him were on the counter. When I asked my mom what had happened, she told me she put him out. She also told him he should stop coming to see me because we all knew I wasn't his real daughter. I immediately ran after him and found him sitting at the bus stop.

To this day, I can remember the sadness in his eyes, and it absolutely broke my heart (and still does when I think about it). In an attempt to have a "mature" conversation and perhaps help prevent issues in the future, I asked my dad why he kept coming to see me and putting up with my mom's drama when I wasn't his real daughter. He firmly looked into my eyes and said, – "You are my daughter! You are my daughter! And I don't ever want to have this conversation with you again." And we didn't!

No matter what he and my mom had going on, he always wanted me to know that I was his daughter and that it was his privilege to share his middle and last name with me. I proudly embraced the names he gave me until the day I got married. I count it as a blessing to be part of his legacy.

Mr. Michael 'Mike' – Bonus Dad

Mike was bold, confident, and had an infectious personality! He was witty and assertive, which made him a natural comedian. He was also loving and generous. From when I was a little girl riding to church with him and his family – until I was pregnant with my own children – I could count on him to go out of  his way to make sure I got things that I needed and wanted. He truly had a heart of gold!

Special Impact Memory

My mom and Mike started dating when I was a baby, and it was told to me by him and his mother (Ms. Peggy McGhee) that once he got his hands on me, he took me home and introduced me to his mother as her 'granddaughter.'

This introduction would prove significant because even after my mom and Mike went their separate ways, my relationship with him, his mom, and his family remained. In fact, I lived with my Grandma Peggy on and off from the time I was an infant until I was in the 5th grade.

When I stayed at Peggy's, Mike would always come by to check on me and allowed me to join him, his wife, and their kids in their family engagements. They would go out of their way on Sunday mornings to come to Peggy's house to take me to church with them, and immediately following church service, I would go to a nice restaurant to eat with their family.

I could share so many other amazing stories about Mike, like how he was the only parental figure who attended my high school graduation or how he always made sure I had the best and most luxurious vehicles when I was traveling back and forth to Seattle to care for my first bonus dad (Tommy Sr.) – and my dad (Tommy) loved every bit of it!

Even though these memories are immensely special to me, there is nothing more special to me than his choosing to make me a part of any family he had. Although he had five beautiful biological children of his own, he never wavered in his stance that I, too, was one of his beautiful daughters!

Mr. George – God-Dad

My God-dad was one of the most  selfless, humble, strong, and supportive men I've ever known. He wasn't a man of many words, but his voice was heard when he spoke, and his message was clear. My God-dad provided stability to his family and many others in more ways than I can explain, but his consistent presence was unmatched by many men of his time. I believe many individuals who lived with my godparents or entrusted them to care for their children would agree that his presence provided us with a special assurance of protection and peace that helped refresh our souls.

Special Impact Memory

I can remember my godparents living in what I would call a 'cozy' two-bedroom home near Judkins Park in Seattle, WA – which was enough space for the two of them and their youngest daughter. But for single mothers like my mom, who struggled a lot with keeping a stable place for us to live and was caught up in the streets, my godparents would open their cozy home up to a boatload of kids.

Now, I'm sure most of the young mothers who needed help would go directly to my god-mom and ask her to watch us for a day or two – but they also knew it would always turn out to be much longer. They would agree to take all of us kids in – often with little to no financial support. I can also recall my god-dad coming home to sometimes one or two extra loud and rumbustious kids, and other times there were five or more of us. I can't recall a time when my god-dad came across as irritated by our presence.

When we would get too unruly, and my god-dad had to set us straight, he was firm but loving. At that point in my life, he was the only man I actually got to see faithfully go to work and come home, which made an imprint on me. I also noticed how he treated my god-mom, which was with great respect from my vantage point. I never saw him disrespect her in any way, which was a new experience for me, especially when I stayed with them after we broke free from my mom's abusive boyfriend, which almost ruined both of our lives. So, seeing a respectful and productive relationship between a man and a woman was rare for me. I was always on alert, waiting to see if something would trigger my god-dad to respond the way I felt like men typically responded (i.e., angry, irritated, etc.). And he never did – thus providing me with a first-time experience of how a man's presence could provide gentle love, peace, and security to a home.

Mr. David Sr. – Dad Hookfin

Dad Hookfin was the epitome of a brilliant, loving, and humble servant-leader. He was a man of great character who had a special way of extending a healthy balance of compassion and course correction to help kids with character development. He knew how to meet us where we were and then challenge us to level up. He  was without question one of the favorites and most respected faculty member during my time at Eckstein Middle School in north Seattle, WA.

Special Impact Memory

I have many memories I could share about the impression that Dad Hookfin had on me, and they all center around three core things: responsibility, accountability, and character development. So, I'll highlight a pivotal 'course correction' moment in my life, a moment when he planted and watered seeds that helped me to grow in all areas of life.

My middle school years were very precarious and a transitional period for me. It was the first time I had lived with my mom full-time, and we both had a lot to learn about life and each other.

There were MANY days that I came to school with a bad attitude or poor disposition because of everything I had going on at home. Anytime Dad Hookfin would catch me in a negative head or emotional space, he would never hesitate to call me into his office to plant and water new 'growth' seeds by initiating candid and often uncomfortable conversations. After I would disclose everything weighing heavy on me, he would lovingly say something like, "Shay, I know you're going through some tough stuff. I get it! Mom Hookfin and I are here to support you as much as we can. But you still have a responsibility to show up for yourself and others with a respectful attitude. And it's not ok to come to school acting any kind of way."

After getting MANY talks, his message became clear to me. He was teaching me to take responsibility for investing in myself and respect the people who were also investing in me despite my circumstances. He helped me process the harsh reality – which was that life had served up tough times to many people, and I was not exempt. In many ways, the wisdom he shared reminded me to acknowledge my feelings and challenged me to decide what experience I wanted to extend to myself and others. He and Mom Hookfin then taught me that I was expected to 'show up' in life. They showed me how servant-leaders courageously extended compassion and course correction to those around them to help them develop a loving character. These lessons have proven to be of great help to me in my own servant-leadership endeavors and growth efforts until this very day.

Mr. Howard – Bonus Dad

Howard was the only bonus dad I lived with full-time before I left for college. He was also the only bonus dad in a relationship with my mom when I lived with her after living with the horrible boyfriend I spoke about in chapter one. Even in all the dysfunction and chaos that was constantly in motion at our house, Howard  and I were able to establish our own special bond.

A few characteristics I admired most about him were that he was direct, protective, and attentive to my needs as a teenager. Whenever I needed something, he would figure out how to make it happen. But I think what I appreciated most about him was that he taught me how to engage in difficult conversations. In the corporate world, we call them 'crucial conversations' – engaging in a dialog when the stakes and emotions are high, but you need to preserve the relationship(s).

He always encouraged me to opine on adult situations that took place in my presence. He also would challenge me to be candid and transparent. He was definitely one of my first communication coaches – and I'm still using the lessons he taught me today!

Special Impact Memory

One of my favorite adventures with Howard was when I was asked to be the MC at a concert during my 8th-grade year at Eckstein Middle School. My mom had started drinking early that day, but Howard decided that he was going to hold off until we went to the concert. When it was time for us to leave for the concert, my mom started acting up, which put us way behind schedule. Since we had to take multiple buses to get to my school, Howard told my mom we were leaving without her – and we did just that. Unfortunately, by the time we got to the bus stop, we had already missed it. As soon as I started to get emotional, Howard looked me in my eyes and said, "Baby, I'm going to get you to that concert! Don't you worry; you're going to be there."

Right after he told me this, we went into a local grocery store, and he asked me to give him a moment. A few minutes later, he introduced me to a lady. He told me that he asked her if she would give us a ride to my concert and she agreed. No more than 20 minutes later we were at the concert – and to my surprise, we were early! He then looked me in the eyes again and said, "Baby, didn't I tell you that I was going to get you here! Didn't I tell you!" I smiled and replied, "Yes, you did!"

Pastor Robert Sr. – God Dad

Humble, brilliant, kind, patient, strong, resilient, and generous are just a few words I would use to describe my god-dad. He is also my first spiritual teacher and counselor. He and my god-mom were the first to entrust me with mature responsibilities I had never had before – which was empowering! He was also the first man to directly confront my  mom and me about the dysfunctional, co-dependent relationship we had and challenged us to acknowledge and address our issues.

Special Impact Memory

One night during my senior year of high school, my mom decided to put me out of her house. Whenever she started drinking, I always knew that there would be drama, which would sometimes lead to her putting me out. But on this night, I was hoping it wouldn't get too bad because my boyfriend didn't realize that she struggled with alcoholism. So, to mitigate the embarrassment, I asked him to go grab us something to eat. But when he returned, she had already started going off and was in the process of putting me out.

Embarrassed and an emotional wreck, I asked him if he could take me to my godparents' house on the other side of town because my mom wouldn't allow me to take my car. When I arrived, my god-dad embraced me and allowed me to weep on his shoulder as if I were a little girl. He then told me to go get some sleep in my god-sister's room, as she was out of town with my god-mom.

Early the next morning, I heard the doorbell, and I knew it was my mom. She had somehow found out where I was. I then heard him tell her how he felt about her behavior and that he would not allow her to mistreat me under his watch. He also told her that he would ask me if I wanted to go with her, but if I didn't want to – she would need to leave. Because of our unhealthy co-dependent relationship, I agreed to go with her. I can vividly remember how he respectfully and firmly confronted my mom about her behavior and how it would not be tolerated moving forward.

Not too long after this incident, my god-dad started 1:1 counseling with me, where we explored the relationship dynamics my mom and I had. I started learning about respectfully setting healthy and loving boundaries through this counseling. I also discovered the counterproductive 'enabling' tendency I had developed that I would spend years correcting. Because my god-dad invested the time to help me learn during this pivotal point in my life, it gave me the courage to do what I believe was necessary to establish a healthier relationship with my mom: the courage to create some distance between us. So, I moved to Texas to start a new chapter of my life. I realized that my mom and I needed healthy and hard-set boundaries, and the distance helped me to establish them. With every fiber of my being, I believe that my move ultimately set us free from the dysfunctional cycle we were both in and helped reset the trajectory for both of our lives – for the good!

Pastor George – God-Dad

Diligent, joyful, caring, humble, gentle, open-minded, selfless, and empathetic are just some attributes that describe my god-dad. I am not the only person who would describe him in this way.

My god-dad's energy is contagious! When he is operating in his gifts of business, teaching, and preaching, it is truly a special sight to witness and experience. But I believe he shines the most in the way he consistently pours out the generous love, joy, compassion, and peace that he provides to his family and to all he loves.

Special Impact Memory

"Let your smile change the world. Don't let the world change your smile."

This quote summarizes the loving message that my god-dad shared with me one difficult Sunday morning in 1996 that has helped me through various seasons of my life.

One Sunday morning, as I stood in the foyer of my church feeling annoyed and overwhelmed after encountering a drama-filled moment with my mom, I noticed my godparents coming my way. As they came closer, I began to smile, but my mom walked up and said something that hit my last nerve, so I stopped smiling.

Once they reached my mom and me, they greeted us with joyful smiles and loving hugs. My mom conversed with them, but I was still annoyed and disengaged. My god-dad then said directly to me – "Where's that bright, beautiful smile? Every time we see you, we say she's always smiling." And even though I didn't feel like smiling, his enthusiasm and joyful expectation were infectious – and it made me smile. I remember even asking myself, "Why are you smiling when you know you're clearly still annoyed?" – but it didn't matter; I kept cheesing from ear to ear and couldn't stop myself.

What I learned that day was that my smile mattered. I also learned that although I couldn't control all the details of my circumstances, I could determine how they impacted me and the energy I extended to others. My god-dad taught me this life-changing lesson not only by being inquisitive but through his actions. His question about my smile was rhetorical – but it was making an important statement that I needed to process. The infectious energy extended by my godparents gave me an unforgettable example and experience about the impor-tance of sharing the love and joy that I have inside despite my circumstances because it's innately a part of me.

Mr. Willie – Uncle Willie

Wise, faithful, loving, humble, provider, and generous perfectly describe my Uncle Willie. He is one of my mom's older brothers, and he and my Aunt were also my mom's parental figures for a short period after my grandmother became ill and was unable to care for her.

For as far back as I can remember, my uncle has been a man of great honor and very loyal to his family. Through the many things my mom put him and my aunt through, they never once failed to do whatever they could to be there for us. My uncle has consistently demonstrated what it looks like to extend unconditional love to family until their days are no more, which he gave to my mom until she took her final breath. He continues to give the same to all of us who are still here.

Special Impact Memory

One day, when I was around ten, my mom was on one of her 'self-sabotage' streaks, so she attempted to steal some clothing items from a department store and return them within a matter of minutes. And, of course, she got caught. When they arrested her, they told her that I was going to CPS. Terrified that she would lose me, she called my uncle, even though she didn't want him to know about some of the things she was doing. And it was a good thing that she did because I can recall hearing conversations about her not being released. Since there was no dad on file for me and no other legal guardian, I would probably go into foster care, which I heard someone say. Shortly after hearing this, I heard someone say that my grandfather was there to pick me up. Since I didn't have any grandparents whom I was familiar with aside from Peggy, I was curious who my mom had found to play the role. When I walked out and saw my uncle standing there, I was immediately at peace. I knew that I was safe and would be okay.

Years later, my uncle and aunt would provide me with the same haven. After I decided to leave Seattle, they graciously opened their home to me. I can't begin to tell you how much of a blessing it was to finally live in a stable home of love, joy, and peace. Living with them gave me a front-row seat to how a husband and wife work together daily – as life partners, co-parents, grandparents, etc. It was a beautiful sight to watch them demonstrate daily how a God-centered marriage worked.

I had no idea that the Lord was going to give me a 'front-row' view of what a healthy, loving, and supportive partnership looked like. I received a visual example of the wisdom and skills needed to build and sustain a marriage. I will never have adequate words to express my gratitude for this God-given experience, as it has definitely been helpful to me throughout my 22 years of marriage.

Mr. Mark – Papa C.

"Coaching is one of the most effective leadership styles – it can transform, empower, and unlock people's potential." - Farshad Asl

Brilliant, tenacious, courageous, confident, and supportive are just some of the characteristics I know and love about my Papa C. I'm not the only one who feels this way about him.

Anytime someone finds out that I've worked with him, the personal stories start flowing. The stories range from him helping to save or catapult someone's career – to helping employees purchase essentials after Hurricane Katrina and helping them write obituaries for loved ones. I love hearing it all because I always find it fascinating that an executive at his level found a way to make personal connections with so many people in so many ways. I find it even more impressive that Papa C continues to nurture and grow the relationships with so many employees even after they left our firm and his retirement. So, I consider myself extremely blessed to have worked under his tutelage as his business protégé and his bonus daughter.

Special Impact Memory

In 2003, as a new management trainee in our firm, I was assigned to develop an 'executive-trainee mentor program' for future program participants. Being in Corporate America was completely new, so I had no idea where to start. But I had been introduced to Papa C through the program leaders, so I decided to ask him if he would partner with me to develop the program – and I was elated when he agreed. He also agreed to be my mentor, so we used our meetings to build the program proposal and for our mentor sessions. In our sessions, he would share practical nuggets of wisdom, and whenever I applied what I learned, I would progress. He was also very direct and didn't hold back from sharing his feedback on areas in which he felt I needed to improve. So, there was never a moment we spent together that I didn't take away learned lessons that were instrumental to my personal and professional growth.

Throughout our time working together, I knew that I had been blessed with a rare gem and a special privilege to be Papa C's mentee. But the moment I felt a special kind of favor was on the night of my program graduation. It was held in Chicago, IL, and we were told that a special award would be presented to the top program graduate. Now, the funny thing is that none of the program participants knew we were being ranked throughout the program until they shared it with us that night. When the time came for the special presentation, they asked for the mystery presenter to come out. When I saw that it was my Papa C, I was shocked and emotionally overwhelmed. I was not only emotional because I was awarded as the top graduate of a program that I didn't ever feel like I was qualified for, but because my mentor made a special trip to help create the special moment. And it was at that moment my mentor, Mr. Mark C, became my Papa C.

Bonus Dads Wrap-up

And there you have it – my AMAZING bonus dad tribe! To all of the generous men who helped restore my heart and refresh my soul with their unconditional love and consistent presence. There are no adequate words to express how THANKFUL I am for each of them. I am determined to live a life with an attitude of GRATITUDE because...

- I am GRATEFUL that these men helped me to revise the narrative about men and dads.
- I am GRATEFUL that even though all my bonus dads had/have their own biological children, they CHOSE to INTENTIONALLY invest in my life.
- I am GRATEFUL to the families of my bonus dads (their wives and children) for allowing me to be part of their lives.
- I am GRATEFUL that I have a restored perspective on love, hope, trust, security, family, and partnership!

Eternally, I am GRATEFUL to the Lord for providing me the 'perfect' bonus dad for each situation and season of my life. I've learned so much from journeying with each of them, as well as from my bonus moms (who are all AMAZING as well, but that's another book!) and all my awesome bonus siblings.

It is said that – "Joy is a gift, and gratitude is a choice." – choosing to share my gratitude daily is easy because I was gifted with my AMAZING Heavenly Pops, bonus dads, and bonus families that have brought a tremendous amount of joy to my life! So, I will forever be GRATEFUL and full of JOY!

My Favorite 'Daddy-Daughter' Lessons

Now that you know more about my AMAZING Heavenly Pops and bonus dads, I want to share some of my favorite 'Daddy-Daughter Lessons' that I learned from them directly and while using some of the principles they shared with me throughout my growth journey. These lessons have helped me be assured in my identity – as a daughter of the King and have empowered me as a servant-leader. I will share my top five favorite lessons, along with some practical insight that helps me make them relevant to all aspects of life.

Lesson #1: Be intentional about exploring, experiencing, and elevating!

Invest time to explore more of the Bible to gain more understanding about our identity so that we can become more aware of who we belong to! Once we understand who we belong to, we can embrace who we are!

- We are image bearers – We are divine, creative, and worthy of awesome things...no matter who our biological parents are!
- We are sons and daughters of the King – Royalty!
- We are FLAWESOME – Yes, we are 'flawed,' but since the Lord's spirit lives in us, we are also 'awesome!'

Once we can acknowledge, accept, and appreciate WHOSE we are and WHO we are – then and only then can we truly begin to experience the abundant life we are promised.

Lesson #2: Be intentional about releasing, rejecting, and renovating!

In all areas that are not serving us and others well, we must keep it real and be ready to:

- Release ALL pain and pleasures (yes - I said, pleasures) that cloud our perspectives.
- Reject all counterproductive thoughts, feelings, emotions, and actions.
- Renovate all areas (spiritual, mental, emotional, and physical) that are needed to ensure that people and things in your environment are 'progressive' and 'fruitful!'

Lesson #3: Be intentional about adjusting thoughts, emotions, and actions!

We have the power to CHOOSE our thoughts, emotions, and actions every minute of every single day – so we must be more deliberate about…

- Reflecting, assessing, and adjusting our thoughts – We really must start 'thinking about what we're thinking about' – and make immediate adjustments as needed. Because the reality is – where the mind goes, the man/woman follows!
- Remember that our feelings do not always have all the right insight to make accurate assessments, so they should never be permitted to be the designated driver in our lives!
- We are dynamic beings with the capacity to share the best parts of ourselves. We must always remember that 'practice makes progress,' and consistent progress creates permanence. Work towards showing up in life as your best self, and refuse the temptation to pursue perfection, as it is impossible to achieve.

Lesson #4: Be intentional about investing and restoring relationships.

We must INVEST in our relationships more carefully because if we don't nourish them, they won't GROW. We should consider how people experience us - and how we experience others. Once we take inventory of our relationships and make the necessary adjustments, we should continue to do the following to help our relationships thrive:

- Work to demonstrate a healthy balance of COMPASSION and CORRECTION toward yourself and others.
- Invest in the right partnerships, do your part, and hold others accountable for doing their part.
- Work on extending GRACE and FORGIVENESS to yourself and others.
- Focus on removing unhealthy expectations placed on us or others.
- Always pursue ways to improve our COMMUNICATION skills – vertical and horizontal!
- Restore relationships by SEEKING OUT ways to connect, collaborate, and create - instead of spending time competing, comparing, and complaining.

Lesson #5: Be intentional about deciding, declaring, discovering, and developing.

- Decide that we do not have to live life like fatherless children!
- Declare the WORD of God over ourselves using scriptures like Psalm 139: 13-16, 1 Corinthians 2:9, Proverbs 31:25, Luke 1:45, Psalm 46:5, Proverbs 3:15-18, Romans 8:31-39, and Jeremiah 29:11. (These are just a few of my

favorites – I encourage you to look them up and incorporate them into your daily affirmations).

- In addition to asking the Lord to be our Savior, we must also ACCEPT His offer to be our Father and then INVITE Him to be our primary life journey partner.
- Remember, God will not force himself or his plan on us. He patiently waits to be CHOSEN by us.
- BELIEVE the Lord wants to be our primary journey PARTNER in life. Believe that he wants to be the ONE who guides and helps us DISCOVER all the GOOD stuff he has inside us and for us!
- Know that he takes JOY in helping us DEVELOP into the BLESSED PEOPLE he designed us to be!

My prayer is that you not only find these lessons to be beneficial but that the experiences that I shared about my Heavenly Pops and bonus dads offer you encouragement. I also pray that you allow yourself to practice these lessons and begin sharing them with your children and the other lives under your sphere of influence.

As I've shared in previous chapters, it is time for all parents to start investing in 'legacy work!' I believe parents and all who are intentional about investing in the care and development of children hold a special place in the Lord's heart. I also believe that He is more than willing to fully equip us with all that we need to walk in our purpose as parents. It's time for us to partner with the Lord, as co-parent partners, and as a community.

Co-Parent Partners – Two individuals who share the responsibilities of raising a child. They are committed to partnering with one another to make the health and well-being of their child(ren) the primary focus.

CHAPTER 5

Co-Parenting Partnerships– It's Bigger Than You

> *"Co-parenting is not a competition. It's a collaboration of two individuals working together with the best interest of the child at heart. Work for your kids, not against them."*
> — Paraphrased, Heather Hetchler

Investing and Pursuing Progress as Co-Parent Partners

The partnership between fathers and mothers is one of the most significant partnerships we'll have in our adult life. And while we all have different family dynamics, there is one common and key factor that we all have as 'humans' – which is the basic need to have parental figures who are present and invested in our growth experience. When parental figures can also commit to partnering with one another to improve the quality of life and secure positive experiences for their child(ren), something truly special happens in the family unit. Co-parent partners must agree to keep the following at the top of their investment priority list:

- Investing in meaningful relationships with your child(ren): Nourish the relationship by consistently providing experiences that are loving, edifying, empowering, connective, and full of other essential support (i.e., spiritual, emotional, mental, financial, etc.).
- Investing in a partnership with each other: Establish a co-parenting partnership that is amicable, respectful, and loving (when possible), incorporating boundaries as appropriate.

It has been proven that 'relationships' and 'partnerships' are 'two peas in a pod.' We sometimes lose sight of the fact that raising, developing, and supporting a child to be a productive member of society is bigger than us. No matter how much we try to sell ourselves, on the 'skewed' narrative that we can raise a child by ourselves, it's simply not true. We all need help in some way, whether we feel like it or not. It's time that we acknowledge that our children and communities would be far better off if we (parental figures) would maximize every opportunity we have to partner and work together to make progress where we can. As we do our work as parents (individuals and partners), we'll begin to see improvements in the physical and social well-being of our child(ren) and communities.

Know Better – Do Better

If we want to truly begin to experience 'sustainable' improvements in our relationships with ourselves, our children, co-parent partners, and others who are important to us, we will have to become more deliberate about our pursuit. We also must accept the reality that when we pursue anything, it takes time and progressive action steps. When we're working on developing meaningful relationships with our child(ren) or co-parent partners, keep in mind that relationships of 'value and substance' require REAL WORK which is consistent, authentic, and selfless. The kind of REAL WORK that doesn't just happen – it requires purposeful investment from all parties involved in the relationship (i.e., parents, children, etc.).

Practice Makes ~~Perfect~~ PROGRESS!

Our progress won't always look graceful, but it's still PROGRESS!

When we are ready to be transparent and honest with ourselves, we will begin acknowledging the various opportunities we have to pursue improvements in the relationships we value most. And when we're really ready to grow, we become more open to exploring different ways to help heal, restore, and build relationships with ourselves, our children, co-parent partners, etc.

When we're truly ready to mature, we pursue ways to better understand how to invest in meaningful relationships. We learn that our investment efforts do not have to be 'grand' or 'perfect' – they just must be genuine, progressive, and consistent!

We must remember that there are NO PERFECT parents, NO PERFECT co-parent partners, and NO PERFECT children! We are all imperfect. In addition to our imperfections, we all have a deep desire to be accepted, loved, and appreciated despite our flaws. But when our flaws bring about hurt and challenges in the lives of the ones we desire to have a relationship with, we cannot afford to ignore or simply provide an explanation to justify behaviors or actions. Take the necessary steps needed to nourish, restore, and preserve relationships. This is why when we "know better - we must do better."

Now, let's explore 'healthy' ways to improve or reconcile relationships with our kids and our co-parent partners since it will not always be a smooth process, especially if the trust has been broken. But just like anything else in life, if we truly want something to improve, it starts with deciding to invest time and effort towards 'practicing' new ways of approaching our relationships.

Next are seven key areas I focus on when I'm working to build a 'new' relationship strengthen or restore 'existing' or old relationships. These seven priorities are foundational to all relationships that are significant to me. It doesn't matter if it's personal or professional relationships. Since we're focused on improving family dynamics, I will keep my points specific to the parent-child relationship and co-parenting partnership.

Important Reminder: As you practice the seven priorities, which are also action steps toward relationship improvements, please be sure to -

- Be 'intentional' about exercising patience through the process

- Challenge yourself to explore ways to increase understanding

- Extend grace to others and yourself

- Practice patience and understanding, extend grace, and establish respectful boundaries.

These will also help mitigate the tendency to get defensive. And keep in mind that anything of significance and worth having takes time...so don't allow time to be a pressure point!

PUTTING TIPS INTO PRACTICE

Next are the foundational tips and techniques that have proven to be beneficial in improving relationships with our children and co-parent partners.

Priority #1: Create a Safe-Brave Space

If we want our children and co-parent partners to become more comfortable with sharing more about their various situations, emotions, and experiences, we have to learn how to create what I like to refer to as a 'safe-brave space.' This is a space where we openly acknowledge for ourselves, our children, and co-parent partners that the information being shared may not be comfortable to deliver or hear. A space where we may feel exposed, vulnerable, fearful, shameful, etc. It also acknowledges that the information being shared requires a tremendous amount of courage because it will challenge us to be transparent, vulnerable, or uncomfortable.

Taking time to engage in discussions in 'safe-brave spaces' will help everyone become more comfortable with the process. Below are some questions that we can include in our discussion process to gain a greater understanding of what makes our children and co-parent partners feel safe:

- What makes you feel 'safe' and 'unsafe' regarding our relationship?
- What do you find most challenging about our relationship – and what provides you comfort?
- Do you feel your voice is heard and your thoughts/ opinions are considered?
- What topics are you uncomfortable talking about?

▪ What can I do to make you feel more comfortable talking about topics you feel can help improve our relationship?

These are just some example questions that you can start with, but be careful not to come across as if you're interrogating them when you're asking these questions. I've been guilty of approaching these conversations incorrectly, and I'm grateful that my kids and co-parent partner don't hesitate to tell me when I'm putting too much pressure on them. Although my intentions may be pure, using the wrong approach and not being open to 'feedback' would've made it impossible for us to make progress.

Priority #2: Listen to Understand – Not to Just Respond

The other thing I had to learn (and I'm still working on) is to do more listening than talking. Our goal is to hear what our kids and co-parent partners are saying, as well as what they may not be saying, – but without making counterproductive assumptions, judgments, accusations, etc.

Attentive listening is also something that doesn't just happen; we have to do it intentionally. If we're honest, most of us (like me) must constantly remind ourselves to keep our mouths closed and listen through conversations. Actively listening is also an essential part of cultivating 'safe-brave spaces.' We want our children and co-parent partners to be their authentic selves while conversing with us without feeling the need to adjust their thoughts to appease us. It would also be a great idea to acknowledge their bravery at each stage of their growth journey. The more we appreciate them for stepping out of their comfort zone to share their thoughts, the more confident and courageous they become.

Lastly, remember that our kids and co-parent partners are not always interested in hearing about what we think they should do or what we did pertaining to what they've shared. *(Lord knows I still struggle with this, but I'm making progress!)* Again, our focus is to create a 'safe-brave' space and listen attentively because the moment is not about us. So, be intentional about getting out of your head so that you can open your ears and heart to truly take in and process the information being shared.

Note: You can ask follow-up questions to gain a better understanding of specific topics that they don't feel comfortable talking about with you specifically. There is a difference between being 'uncomfortable' talking about topics in general versus talking about specific topics with you. Again, this would not be the time for you to take offense. Simply see if they are willing to help you grow together in this space if possible. Sometimes, people just feel more comfortable talking about certain topics with certain parental figures, which is all good as long as you know the adult figure has a healthy perspective to share.

Priority #3: Be Willing to Initiate and Engage in Uncomfortable Conversations

Healing 'visible' and 'invisible' wounds from our life journey is never easy. It will take everything we have to address the pain, brokenness, disappointments, rejections, failures, shame, and trauma within ourselves – and it will be worth everything we have to heal and grow.

Initiating and engaging in uncomfortable conversations can trigger emotions and thoughts we didn't even know were buried inside us. However, it's impossible to have authentic and lasting relationships if we're unwilling to engage in uncomfortable conversations. We must have regular dialog with our children and co-parent partners on all topics, especially topics that could potentially hinder our relationships.

If I haven't learned anything else from life, I've learned that it's important for everyone to constantly develop their communication and comprehension validation skills. The more we learn how to initiate and engage in effective conversations, the more likely we'll be able to handle uncomfortable conversations more successfully. Improving our communication skills not only preserve the relationships but make them stronger.

One of my favorite books is titled *Crucial Conversations: Tools for Talking When Stakes are High* by Kerry Patterson, Joseph Grenny, Ron McMillan, and Al Switzler. I read this book when I joined the firm I work for in 2003 as a trainee in a management development program. Our leaders had us read this book for many reasons that were spot-on and extremely helpful to us as future leaders in the corporate world. But when I read the insight shared in this book, I could also see how the principles shared could be applied to any space or relationship – professionally and personally. Once I coupled what I learned from this book with the 'life' lessons I'd learned growing up, I started to see how essential and valuable 'crucial conversations' were to all my relationships.

Now, I initiate and engage in crucial conversations when:

■ Stakes are high

■ Emotions are high

■ And I desire to preserve the relationship

Once I started practicing some of the communication principles and techniques I learned, not only in my professional spaces but in my personal relationships, I became a better communicator. Part of improving my communication also included improving my 'listening' skills and becoming more reflective of the experiences I provided and encountered.

I realize that I'm sharing a lot of information, and my prayer is that you're still pacing with me because all that I'm sharing truly works together. This insight being shared are lessons learned and best practices I use that changed my life and many others. Throughout my entire life, I've not only witnessed poor relationship management and communication skills, but I've also experienced my share of 'superficial' relationships. But once I decided to be intentional about pursuing whatever development I needed to make progress, I got to work – and I'm still working! No one is exempt from being my practice partner – my husband, kids, mom, extended family, friends, colleagues, etc.

The way I see it, we have countless instances in our lives where:

- The *stakes become high* – ex. We lose the opportunity to have a healthy relationship with our children, co-parent partners, or anyone we desire to be in our lives.
- The *emotions become high* – ex. When we don't see eye-to-eye with our co-parent partners, and we can't seem to get over ourselves to do what's in the best interest of our children.
- *Preserving the relationship in jeopardy* – ex. The behaviors and actions we demonstrate make it challenging to maintain a loving, respectful, and peaceful relationship with the ones we love most.

My point is – initiating and engaging in 'crucial conversations' is an essential part of any relationship we have as individuals, family units, and professionals. So, it is in our best interest to pursue whatever development we can, practice what we learn whenever we can and make as much progress as we can! So, pursue…practice…progress…and REPEAT!

Priority #4: Find A 'Wise' Sounding Board

If you're new to initiating or effectively engaging in uncomfortable (crucial) conversations, I'd highly recommend seeking out a 'wise' sounding board. A sounding board is a person(s) we can share our thoughts on how we have or plan to approach a situation, and they listen and help us sort through the information we share. My only word of caution is for you to be very discretionary about who you allow to be your sounding board, especially when you're working through relationship topics concerning your co-parent partner, child(ren), or any relationship you value. If you've already encountered a crucial conversation and aren't sure it went well, I'd advise you to leverage a sounding board as well. Personally, I am VERY particular about who I select as a sounding board for me, especially regarding matters of the heart and the relationships with my kids, husband, and other loved ones– for several reasons:

- #1: Not everyone knows how to extend empathy or can demonstrate the courage necessary to share course corrections.
- #2: It's important that I share similar views on integrity and character with the person I get feedback from (i.e., insight, advice, etc.) for consistency.
- #3: It's important that they are discretionary, especially if I specifically ask for confidentiality. Everything is not for public consumption or opinion.

As I shared in previous chapters, I'm an advocate for seeking professional counsel, but I also believe in establishing a 'wise' small network of sounding boards if you can.

Priority #5: Establish Healthy Boundaries

Healthy boundaries and respectful engagement practices are mission-critical to making progress on any of the topics. When establishing boundary agreements and engagement practices (i.e., overreacting, withdrawing, etc.), it is extremely vital that we do what we say we're going to do - NO MATTER WHAT! Adherence to the agreement is critical, whether the agreement is made with a child or a co-parenting partner. We should always know that as parents, our kids will always hold us accountable for doing our part, even if they do not do theirs. The blessing is that when we stay committed to doing our part, we gain their trust and become an 'example' they can learn from.

Priority #6: Conduct Impact Assessments Regularly

To help us on growth journeys as parents and co-parent partners, I would HIGHLY recommend that we learn how to perform a proper impact assessment of our behaviors and actions – ideally before they're in motion. Failing to invest proper time in considering what our decisions can cost us and our families can be devastating.

A valuable strategy I've incorporated into both my personal life and professional endeavors, drawing from my experiences in business school and the corporate world, is known as the "S.W.O.T. Impact Assessment." S.W.O.T. is an acronym for *Strengths, Weaknesses, Opportunities, and Threats.*

I have chosen to use it to improve my relationships by simply asking myself the following questions:

- *Strengths*: What strong areas exist in my relationships? Are my strengths being leveraged to support the relationships I desire to have with the ones I love most?
- *Weaknesses*: What weaknesses exist in my relationships? How are my behaviors or actions counterproductive to the relationships I value most?
- *Opportunities:* What opportunities exist or can be created to help my relationships flourish?
- *Threats:* What threats exist that can hinder the relationships I value most?

Again, these are just examples of some of the questions I include in my assessment process. Although this might seem like a lot, I can truly say I don't ever think about the time it takes to perform my assessments because it has become so natural. I sincerely want all of the people I love and value most to be at the forefront of my mind constantly. I want to explore ways to help me learn and grow as an individual, parent, co-parent partner, etc., and challenge myself to truly invest time into assessing the impact of my behaviors and actions. Having a better understanding of all the things I do have the power to control or influence has REALLY helped me grow in more ways than I have time to share. But I do want you to take a moment to think about the following questions:

- What if we (parents) were more intentional about doing our own 'Impact/S.W.O.T. Assessments' when it came to the decisions we make as individual parents and as co-parent partners about all topics that impact the lives of our children?
- What if we (parents) got really honest and transparent with ourselves – could we say that we would be happy to have our children mirror the same behaviors and/ or actions that we display towards them, our co-parent partners, or others?
- If our children grew up to be an identical reflection of us, would we like the image mirrored?

Priority #7: Practice Makes ~~Perfect~~ PROGRESS – Practice, Practice, Practice!

All the tips and techniques shared have not only helped me but they've also humbled me tremendously as a parent and co-parent partner. They remind me that being a parent and a co-parent partner is NO JOKE, takes a TON of practice, and is a LIFE-LONG learning lesson! And in addition to learning about how to best nurture and support our children as a parent, we are also learning about our 'co-parent partnership' role simultaneously!

As we learn about ourselves and our co-parent partners in our lead roles, we quickly discover that although we'll get some things right, there will be a TON we get wrong. Trying to raise children, partner with someone on the same parenting learning path as you, and manage other roles and responsibilities in life can be overwhelming, even if there's no added 'drama.' So when there is added drama, dysfunction, and relational disconnections, things get even more complicated!

As we've already established, there are no "perfect" families, parents, co-parents, children, etc. – all humans are works in progress. The sooner we realize that we are all learning and growing as we go, the sooner we can begin to extend grace to others and ourselves. Please remember perfection is both 'elusive' (difficult to achieve) and 'illusive' (deceptive).

Please remember that we (parents) are never too old to learn and practice new ways of doing things. Our kids can benefit from learning from our experiences more effectively when we are consistently pursuing and practicing behaviors and actions that will help improve their experiences with us as parents and co-parent partners. Please remember that sustainable progress takes time, and mistakes will be encountered. But it's ALL GOOD because success and mistakes can help us grow if we allow them to! So, press forward and stay focused!

"FOCUS ON WHAT'S IMPORTANT, CAPTURE THE GOOD TIMES... DEVELOP FROM THE NEGATIVES, AND IF THINGS DON'T WORK OUT, TAKE ANOTHER SHOT!"
– ZIAD K. ABDELNOUR

Each moment of each day, we all have REAL opportunities to make NEW decisions that have the power to change the entire trajectory of our lives and those connected to us.

CHAPTER 6

Opportunities and Decisions— Grace and Growth Required

"Many believe parenting is about training children to become adults or even controlling their behaviors and lives. But what parenting should really be about is controlling our own behaviors and acting like adults ourselves. Because the reality is our children learn what they live and live what they learn."

Paraphrased Quote by L.R. Knost

Dads Choose Wisely

In this chapter, we will discuss two critical areas that we (parents) have before us daily – opportunities and decisions. In order to make real, sustainable, and positive changes in raising our children, we must acknowledge the growth opportunities we have as parents and co-parent partners. As long as we are alive, we will always have the following:

- We will have *opportunities* to grow by taking advantage of the opportunities extended to us or the ones we create for ourselves.
- *Decisions* that we'll have to make – and others that we will need to respond to.
- **Results**/outcomes we'll have to process and manage.

Life has taught most of us that managing opportunities and decisions can be immensely challenging. Sometimes, we'll maximize our opportunities nicely, and the decisions that we make will result in success. But other times, we'll jack up a rare opportunity and make the worst decisions. However, an awesome reminder I like to share with myself and others daily is this: –

Each moment of each day, we all have REAL opportunities to make NEW decisions that have the power to change the entire trajectory of our lives and those connected to us. Although the transition phase experienced going from 'old' to 'new' may not always be easy and may take longer than we desire, we can be assured that progress is occurring, and progress is always a step in the right direction!

Since we've already covered a great deal of insight pertaining to how co-parent partners can maximize opportunities and improve decision-making, we will now highlight some specifics for dads and moms. Here are two prayers for dads and moms. My prayer is that both will invest time to read, not only to use in your own personal growth journey but to also share with others along theirs. I also pray that you decide to be self-reflective, encouraged, and empowered to take the necessary steps for improvement.

Dear Dads (Biological and Bonus):

First, I would like to give a special shout-out to all the men who are currently intentional about their roles and responsibilities as fathers. AWESOME JOB - keep up the AMAZING work! Please remember that other men struggle in various areas of fatherhood and co-parenting and could benefit from the insight you can share. I would challenge you to maximize any opportunities to share lessons learned and best practices with these dads or dads-to-be. And if the opportunity for you to share and encourage is not immediately apparent – create an opportunity and make it happen!

Now, if you're a dad who is not doing well in the spaces of fatherhood or co-parenting, you have a special opportunity to course correct! You can make a narrative adjustment to your story, your child(ren)'s story, and your co-parent partner's story. You have an opportunity to begin or continue creating a lasting legacy full of GREATNESS, but you will have to be tenaciously deliberate. You must commit to investing time into learning more about yourself, your children, and others who play key roles in your family dynamics. And last, and most importantly – you will have to commit to developing loving and respectful relationships.

Here are some key reminders that will help you on your growth journey:

- Trading your 'expectations' for 'gratitude' will help a ton in your growth process! When we demonstrate an attitude of gratitude even when situations are not ideal, it has the power to shift everything! Plus, it helps to prevent the 'bruised ego syndrome' that often sabotages progressive efforts.
- You don't have to be perfect, but you do need to be consistently 'present' – spiritually, emotionally, mentally, and physically.
- Practice makes progress - Be practical and patient with yourself and others!

Also, remember to conduct regular personal assessments of your thoughts and emotions. Maintaining a 'realistic' perspective of what's happening inside of you will definitely help you better gauge how others are experiencing you – especially your babies. It's hard to establish or strengthen connections with the people you love when you have so many unaddressed thoughts and emotions. So please, take the time to ask yourselves some REAL questions, and allow yourselves to respond HONESTLY!

- Are you, or have you been, afraid of your feelings?
- Are your emotions the designated driver in your relationship? And if they are, do you know how to get the keys back?

- Are you, or have you been, a slave to your pride?
- Does your unchecked ego go rogue, putting you and your relationships in precarious situations?

These are just some questions you should ask yourselves. I would also encourage you to not only have this conversation with yourself but also encourage you to allow someone to help you. We've already acknowledged the difficulty men experience seeking out help. But because I have faith that you all have what it takes to do 'your work,' I'm still going to encourage you to challenge yourself to step out of your comfort zone. As you challenge yourself to explore something new, embrace all of the strength, courage, and maturity that will surely come with it.

Again, if you are struggling to really sort through your thoughts, emotions, and actions, please give yourself permission to get help. Professional counseling can be accessed in many ways. Know that most people don't initially feel comfortable reaching out or accepting help. But if we're keeping it 100% – we teach our kids to ask for help when they need it. So, I'm simply reminding you to practice what you probably preach. Give them a 'real' and 'personal' example of what it's like to seek out and receive help in a way that will address/resolve the 'root' of a problem. Teach them that problems don't age well by showing them that you are willing to do whatever it takes to address issues, emotions, past traumas, and anything else that could potentially create disconnects in your relationship and disrupt a powerful legacy! You are purposed to create!

The Time is NOW!

Pour all your investments into building a legacy of love, strength, peace, and courage for your children. Create a legacy that will remain past your days, has the power to positively influence people you may never know, and impact places you may never go!

Lastly, if you know your relationship with yourself, your child(ren), and/or co-parent partner could be better, then acknowledge that you must make the **decision** daily to...

- *Evolve* - Begin investing in you, your children, and the legacy that will continue to flow through them. **(Opportunity)**

- *Repeat* – Keep doing what you've always done and rob yourself and your child(ren) of experiencing the BEST parts of you. **(Option)**

At the end of this book, you will find a section titled 'I.D. Encouragement Keys' (I.D. - Intentional Dads), which has some recommended resources for you to check out. I highly encourage you to allow yourself to use these resources – the affirmations, book recommendations, and the playlist. I'm optimistic that this will help encourage you as you work to maximize opportunities and make better decisions!

"Navigating being a good father and man while trying to rid our mind of past behaviors and anguish inside is a daily fight! Keep Going, Fellas! Whether you're in the fight with a significant other or single – Keep Going!"

– Mr. Enye Dinish

Dear Moms (Biological and Bonus):

I was blessed to grow up around many strong, courageous, and strategic women, so I did a lot of observing. There are some situations that I observed and decided to apply in my own life that proved to be to my detriment. And many lessons learned that I applied in my life that served me well. A few basic but extremely important truths I learned are –

- We (moms) have the power to be a 'help' or a 'hindrance' in the relationship between a father and his children.
- If we (moms) really want our efforts/contributions to be fruitful, we must be completely honest with ourselves about what our 'true' intentions are when it comes to our contributions toward the 'father-child' relationship. Because when we get down to the nitty-gritty, most of the time, we know exactly when we are a 'help' or a 'hindrance' in a relationship.
- We (moms) also have the daily opportunity to 'evolve' and make more fruitful investments toward the 'father-child' relationship. I am not suggesting that you share

any 'fabricated' information with your children or co-parent partners. I'm simply encouraging you to be more intentional about your contributions. Before you proceed with any actions that could affect the relationship, consider whether they will yield positive results or prove to be costly and counterproductive.

If you are a mom who is currently intentional about fostering positive relationships between fathers and their children – AWESOME JOB! Please continue doing what you're doing! And please do what you can to share best practices and lessons learned with other ladies who might be struggling in this area. If you admit that you are not currently doing what you can to nurture and support the relationship between your children and their fathers, I commend you for being honest with yourself and challenge you to do some course correcting. Course correction seems to work best when we –

- can be honest with ourselves
- extend ourselves and other's grace
- make a commitment to change our course of action in an area that hasn't served us or others well (especially our kids)

One of my favorite phrases is "It's all good!" – simply because most things have a way of working out to be 'lessons' or 'blessings.' And if we really think about it, most 'lessons,' even the difficult ones, teach us something that can help us, our children, and others.

I believe most mothers truly want the best for their children – we do not want them to be affected or infected by our trauma or drama, even though it still might happen. Unfortunately, while trying to figure out how to safeguard ourselves and our children from continuing unhealthy cycles, we can sometimes lose sight of how counterproductive our behavior and actions are. We can also lose sight of how impressionable our children are. We can forget how in tune our children are with our emotions and how they watch our actions like a hawk.

They even see the emotions we so desperately try to hide. So, please remember that our children use their 'eyes, ears, and feelings' to create their own narratives about the relationship dynamics within the family unit. These narratives then shape their experience – influencing and impacting their entire life story.

The bottom line, Moms, is we play a huge role in shaping our kids' views and narratives – especially regarding relationship dynamics. If we're not careful and if we're not INTENTIONAL about how we handle this area, especially when it comes to relationships between our kids and their dads, we can be doing more harm than good.

So, when I say that we – as mothers – can either 'help' or hinder' – I'm truly not trying to 'over-simplify' the layered and complex situations we sometimes encounter. I'm simply challenging us to establish a 'simplified' way to be more insightful and self-reflective so that we can easily course-correct ourselves. We need to be able to honestly and quickly assess if our behaviors/actions will...

▪ *Help* to support 'progressive' and 'productive' out-
comes and dynamics in our relationships (which may
not always feel comfortable or easy for all parties).

▪ *Hinder* our children's overall well-being, the relationship between them and their father(s), or any relationship dynamics that might impact our children's overall
growth journey and life experiences.

Ladies, the choice is really ours. We just need to acknowledge that our decisions involve, impact, and influence others.
So, it's best for us to reference and use the 'Impact Assessment'
approach mentioned earlier in Chapter 5. The great thing
about taking the time to do a 'personal' assessment before acting on anything is that it always creates the best chance for us
to apply lessons learned and maximize the growth moments.
In other words, it demonstrates that when we know better, we
have the best chance of doing better!

In closing, moms, I encourage you to read the following
poem and really take time to process each word. The poem
is titled "The Touch of a Woman," and it was written by a
dear family friend, Mr. Gerald Green, some time ago. The title
alone captured my attention when he shared it with me. It resonated with me on so many levels, especially as I spent time
listening to the fathers I had the opportunity to interview. As
I allowed myself to digest the words shared, I thought about
what I learned during the interviews, the exposure I've had
to 'healthy' and 'unhealthy' relationships and considered my
own improvement opportunities. It resulted in me challenging myself to 'level-up.'

The Touch of a Woman

The touch of a woman is more than her caress –
it is all in her speech, nothing more, nothing less.

Respectful and loving, should be her main goal –
and encouraging men to honor his role.

Her tongue, like a knife can maim and kill.
But the tongue of a woman can also soothe and heal.

Her tongue like a fist can make a man cry.
The tongue of a woman can also lift a man high.

The touch of a woman, so sweet and so warm.
Her shelter of love can be his peace in the storm.

The touch of a woman is more than her caress -
it is all in her speech, nothing more, nothing less.

Written by: Mr. Gerald Green

Ladies, we are so powerful, and of course, I know this, but the poem challenged me to also think about the responsibility that comes with such power. It made me get really honest with myself about how I was using the power I was blessed with. It challenged me to reflect on times when I used my power to 'build up' others and the times I used it to 'tear down' – directly and indirectly. I decided that although I would never be 'perfect,' I could be more intentional about improving how I conducted myself.

I'm sharing all this to remind you that you, too, must take time to acknowledge your power, reflect on how you've used it in the past, think about your sphere of influence, and what adjustments will be needed for you to ensure fruitful results. We must decide to use our power to help create and nurture relationships in a way that is full of 'beauty' – instead of allowing children to pick up learned behaviors that have the potential of starting and fueling 'battles' in their future relationships.

Now, Moms, I extend the same challenge that I presented to the dads – which is for you to become more intentional about how you move forward, not only as a mom but as a co-parenting partner. And I pray that you allow the message in this section and the other insight shared throughout this book to help you along your continued growth journey.

Extend Grace as We Go and Grow

I said it before, and I'll say it again - parenting is hard work! And a co-parent partnership is not for the faint of heart. So, lets just decide to extend a generous dose of "grace" to ourselves and co-parent partner along our journey. Parenting and co-parent partners will challenge us daily to deal with our inadequacies, insecurities, selfishness, immaturity, etc. And when we choose not to deal with them, they come back for us to deal with at another inconvenient time. So, I simply would like to encourage you to deal with whatever comes up, and when you do, be willing and ready to extend grace. Remember, problems don't age well – and with all that comes with being a parent, a co-parenting partner, and just a person in general, we truly don't have the capacity to keep unresolved issues in constant rotation in our lives. We really should want to avoid passing any unresolved generational issues to our babies. It will take us working together to make progress, and grace can be the key ingredient to bring everything together.

With all the mess I've been through, I knew that my decision-filtering process was tainted, so I didn't always trust myself to make progressive decisions. So, I asked the Lord to teach me how to be a good mother, co-parent partner, friend, wife, etc. And I continue to do so every day! With His help, I can honestly say that I've learned the importance of embracing and extending grace to myself and others – with necessary boundaries. Taking the time to acknowledge our outlook on parenting and partnership, being honest in areas that need to be addressed, and then taking the steps necessary to make improvements will determine how well we'll operate in each role. As shared several times before, the goal is not to be 'perfect' parents or partners – it's simply to be progressive!

The funny thing is that we (parents) sometimes forget that when we decide to have children with someone, we automatically decide to be in a partnership with that person. And at the center of our partnership is our child(ren). Like any other joint venture/partnership, it requires that we figure out how to effectively communicate, commit to equal contribution, and prioritize our investment (i.e., our children). If you know anything about strong and successful joint ventures, you know that there's a level of trust, understanding, grace, and loyalty that is established at some point.

How powerful would it be to provide our kids with 'practical' lessons to help them in their future relationships – friendships, romantic, parental, boss and subordinate, etc.? How beneficial would it be for our kids to learn that we were designed to do life together and that we're not only capable of doing it – we were built to do it and do it effectively? How much would the family unit grow if we decided to incorporate the exchange of grace in our co-parent partnership?

I love what Ecclesiastes 4:9-12 says about the power of partnership:

"Two are better than one because they have a good return for their labor; If either of them falls down, one can help the other up. But pity anyone who falls and has no one to help them up. Also, if two lie down together, they will keep warm. But how can one keep warm alone? Though one may be overpowered, two can defend themselves. A cord of three strands is not easily broken."

With all that is happening in the world today, our children NEED strong and supportive foundations, which we should always strive to provide. To elevate our 'co-parent partnerships' and help our kids thrive – we'll have to be more intentional about exchanging GRACE, which automatically turns into a growth moment. Exchanging the gift of grace is also an amazing way to teach our kids how to extend love and respect even when a person is flawed (as we all are). We can demonstrate to them how extending grace must also include boundaries based on the maturity of the people we're dealing with.

Together, there is NO DOUBT that we can encourage, educate, empower, and ultimately elevate the experience and conversations regarding the 'co-parent partnership'!

Grace Exchange Growth Challenge – Are You Ready?

Before we wrap up, I must conclude with a final growth challenge.

Stop, Start, and Continue Exercise Instructions:

Simply write down 2-3 responses for the following questions:

1. What do I need to '**stop**' doing that is hindering my growth and my relationships with others (i.e., my kids, co-parent partner, etc.)?
2. What do I need to '**start**' doing that will help me grow and my relationships with others improve?
3. What should I '**continue**' doing that is helping me and my relationships progress?

If you really want to take your 'growth' to the next level, ask your kids, co-parent partners, spouses, close friends, counselor, etc., to complete these exercise questions. Ask them to be transparent and honest. They can either share their responses with you verbally or in writing. Your response must simply be 'Thank You.' You cannot explain, be combative, or give off vibes of annoyance or anger.

Again, we don't do life alone; we do it with others and need them to help us better understand how we are being externally experienced. Despite good intentions and our best efforts, we can get things wrong – and we need others to feel 'safe' sharing feedback with us so that we can course-correct.

The objective is to be keenly aware of 'growth' opportunities – especially if they help you create a better life for yourself, your family, and others around you.

Be Encouraged – YOU GOT THIS!

Thank you again for investing time to absorb the insights shared throughout this chapter – and the entire book. I pray that you are encouraged to use the information and challenges. I pray you always remember that we put ourselves, our children, and our co-parent partners in the best position when we decide to be intentional about our growth journeys. And please remember....

■ There is no such thing as a "perfect" parent or co-parent partner – so just be real ones who are maximizing growth opportunities and making better decisions!

▓ Children need and deserve the care, love, presence, support, and overall investment of both parents.

▓ We can be flawed and awesome parents at the same time – it's called *"Flawesome Parenting."* We just have to be in constant pursuit of progress for the well-being of ourselves and our families.

▓ Never stop being INTENTIONAL about...
  * *Exercising* patience
  * *Exploring* ways to increase your understanding
  * *Extending* grace
  * *Embracing* growth opportunities

Always remember that the Lord is also an AMAZING Father (Abba) and co-parent partner with a wealth of experience, and He's always willing and ready to do life with you!

"Being a good co-parent means putting your child's needs first, even when it's difficult. It's about providing a consistent and loving presence in their life."
- Mahershala Ali

CHAPTER 7

I.D. (Intentional Dads) Encouragement Keys

"Promise me that you'll always remember that you're braver than you believe, stronger than you seem, and smarter than you think."

— *Christopher Robin*

I know that you might think it's kind of corny to use a quote from *Winnie the Pooh,* but if you really allow yourself to embrace the message, you will understand how power-ful it is. The most significant battles we face as people take place in our 'minds.' And since part of my divine assignment is to remind you that you are already equipped with what you need to be successful in every role the Lord allows you to serve in, this section is purposed to do just that! It includes 'key' resource references that will help keep you encouraged! You will find positive affirmations for dads, a recommended 'life music' playlist, and powerful book recommendations.

I sincerely believe all of these resources have the power to restore and empower your souls, hearts, and minds!

Positive Affirmations for Dads

Incorporating positive affirmations into your everyday life is an excellent way to invest in yourself and your children. Affirming yourself in a healthy and humble way has the power to change your life in ways you can't even begin to imagine! One of my favorite quotes is, *"Change your thoughts – Change your world!"* – It has proven to be true in my life, as well as many others I know. When we invest time to affirm ourselves in positive ways, we are giving ourselves the love that we need to care for and love others. It helps us to reprogram our minds productively and can manifest positive improvements in our feelings, actions, and experiences.

To get you started, I've pulled together a few positive affirmations you can speak to yourself daily:

1. I am full of purpose and power – which means I am equipped with everything I need to create blessings to pass on to my kid(s).
2. It's not too late for me to become a better dad.
3. I am capable of building a legacy of love.
4. My kid(s) do not need me to be 'perfect;' they need me to be 'present,' and I am capable of becoming the dad they need and deserve.

5. I am grateful for the opportunity to be a dad to my kid(s).
6. I appreciate the time that I get to spend with my kid(s).
7. I am capable of being intentional in everything I do – which means that I can build and sustain meaningful relationships with my kid(s) and my co-parent partner.

Your Turn!

It's time to create affirmations for yourself in the space provided below.

POSITIVE AFFIRMATIONS
FOR DADS

Personal Growth Exercise: In the section below, I challenge you to write down your top five affirmations that encourage you, speak them aloud to yourself daily – multiple times a day if you desire – and, most importantly, EXPECT them to become evident in your life.

1.

2.

3.

4.

5.

Quick Tip: If you're interested in easily incorporating 'positive affirmations' in your life, try downloading an application on your phone. My current favorite is the "I AM – Daily Affirmations, Positive Reminders Motivation" app. I love it because it always seems to send me loving reminders exactly when I need them. I highly recommend that you explore new resources and ways to keep yourself encouraged.

Life Music Playlist – More Than Just a Melody

Music is POWERFUL! It has a way of captivating our hearts and minds in ways human beings cannot do through spoken words. Music has an unexplained power to influence us from the inside out. Those who know me will tell you that I LOVE music, especially when the lyrics are richly laced – healing and empowering the souls that embrace the message being shared. I call this kind of music "Life Music."

I refer to some music as "Life Music" because it does exactly that. It gives me life, especially when I'm in a headspace that's not the best, and I may not know how to get myself out of a funk. There are songs I can play that help change my entire outlook and bring a certain peace to my mind. As I've gotten older, I've come to REALLY understand the importance of REALLY listening to lyrics and seeing how they impact me.

So, I felt led to share some songs that I believe have powerful and encouraging messages for all who will listen to them – but I also believe there is a special message for dads and men! The songs included remind us that we are loved unconditionally and capable of walking out our purpose – with our flaws and all!

I sincerely hope you take the time to 'intentionally' listen to each song. And just like some of us had to do back in the day when we couldn't easily 'skip' over the songs we didn't like (LOL) – go ahead and listen to the entire playlist, and then you can select your favorites. I would love to know which songs resonated with you, so hit me up on social media (FB or IG) and let me know.

PLAYLIST

	Song Titles	Artist Names	Album Names
1	A Whole Nation	Kirk Franklin	Fight of My Life
2	Success Is in Your Hand Fred Hammond & Radical for Christ	The Spirit of David	(Psalm 34:4,5)
3	Intentional	Travis Greene	The Hill
4	No Gray	Jonathon McReynolds	Life Music
5	The Curse Is Broken	James Fortune & FIYA	Identity
6	Cycles	Jonathon McReynolds	Make More Room
7	Just for Me	Kirk Franklin	Long Live Love
8	Lovin' Me	Jonathan McReynolds	Life Music
9	Being with You	Marcus Cole	Write My Song
10	Father Knows Best	Kirk Franklin	Long Live Love
11	Worth Fighting for	Brian Courtney Wilson	Worth Fighting For - Live
12	Movin' On	Jonathon Mc Reynolds & Mali Music	People

Empowerment Book Resources

The Tony Evans Study Bible – Christian Standard Bible, TONY EVANS
*Important Note: If not this one, a Study Bible you enjoy – just get one!

What is the Father Like – A Devotional Look at How God Cares for His Children, W. PHILLIP KELLER

Of Boys and Men – Why the Modern Male is Struggling, Why it Matters, and What to Do About It, RICHARD V. REEVES

Male vs. Man, DONDRE' WHITFIELD

Time with God for Fathers, JACK COUNTRYMAN

The Father You've Always Wanted – How God Heals Your Father Wounds, ED TANDY MCGLASSON

Do It Afraid – Embracing Courage in the Face of Fear, JOYCE MEYER

The 7 Habits of Highly Effective People, STEPHEN R. COVEY

The Power of Vulnerability, BRENE BROWN

Until We Reconnect...

I would like to THANK YOU again for the investment you made to read this book, and I pray that all of the insight shared proves to be of great encouragement to you.

In closing, I'll leave you with one more 'loving reminder' from scripture that will help you keep your mind and actions focused as you press forward toward progressing personally, as a parent, and co-parenting partner.

"Finally, brothers and sisters, whatever is true, whatever is noble, whatever is right, whatever is pure, whatever is lovely, whatever is admirable – if anything is excellent or praiseworthy – think about such things. Whatever you have learned, received, or heard from me or seen in me – put it into practice. And the God of peace will be with you."

– Philippians 4: 4-9 (NIV)

Special Thanks

"No one who achieves success does so without acknowledging the help of others. The wise and confident acknowledge this help with gratitude."

— Alfred North Whitehead

I want to give special thanks to the many AMAZING individuals who were instrumental in helping me birth this divine assignment. Thank you to:

My Heavenly Pop, Bonus Dads, and Dad Interviewees: Even though I dedicated the entire 'Special Acknowledgment' section at the beginning of the book to thank you, I just wanted to say it again. THANK YOU for the time shared and investments made to help me complete this divine assignment. I truly couldn't have done it without all of you!

My Handsome Man: "The quality of a father can be seen in the goals, dreams, and aspirations he sets not only for himself but for his family." – Reed Markham

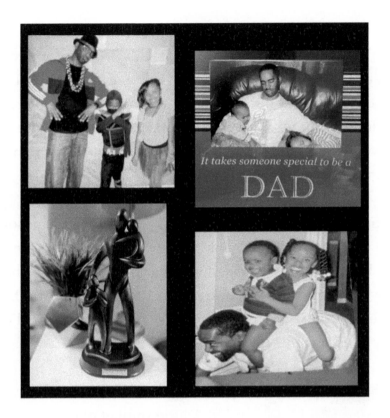

Oh, how this quote reminds me so much of you, my love. From the time we started our family, your vision and desires for our family were greater than I could even comprehend at the time. Your ingenuity, courage, resilience, and strength were all qualities that provided me with the confidence and security that I needed to follow your lead. Your commitment to demonstrating these same qualities, along with the consistent love and support that you lavish our kids with, makes you a PHENOMENAL DAD. Thank you for also being the BEST co-parent partner and husband! I have thoroughly enjoyed doing life with you! It's truly been an IMMENSE pleasure having a front-row view of your fatherhood journey. Thank you for always providing me with a space of abundant LOVE, ENCOURAGEMENT, PEACE, and SUPPORT! I am SO GRATEFUL for our friendship, partnership, and marriage relationship. Building such a purposed-filled crew with our Heavenly Pops and you have, without question, been one of my greatest accomplishments!

My Sweetfaces: To my beautiful girl (Asia) and my handsome little fellow (Jaden) – Thank you for bringing me so much JOY. It has truly been a blessing to be your mommy, as I have enjoyed being a part of every aspect of your life. You both make me so very proud, and I KNOW that our Heavenly Pops has placed greatness inside both of you.

My Mom - Mrs. Vivian: Mommy, we did it! A little snippet of our story has finally been captured in a book like you always used to say. You and I both know that I just scratched the surface of the various peaks and valleys of our testimony, but I'm optimistic that what we've shared will help someone. It has been more than ten years since I've been able to speak with you and share my gratitude. I'm grateful for the opportunity to be your daughter and for our growth journey together. It wasn't always ideal, but there's no doubt that it helped me develop into the woman I am today. Thank you for always demonstrating complete confidence in my ability to LEVEL

UP and BLOOM wherever I was planted. I know you know that I will continue to do my best to represent you, my bonus dads, and our Heavenly Pops well! I miss you and love you very much always.

My Bonus Moms and Siblings: Thank each of you for your loving embrace. You didn't have to share your husbands and dads with me or welcome me into your families, but you did! My life was blessed because you did. So, thank you for your selflessness, compassion, and for always making me feel like I had a place in your family.

My Special Gem - Sarah Hall: To my sweet and beautiful little sister, you are a 'true' blessing in more ways than I'll ever be able to adequately express. So, I simply say – THANK YOU for investing in me and my family so generously! Thank you for encouraging me and helping me acquire everything I needed to move forward with my divine assignment. I will forever be grateful to our Heavenly Pops for your brilliant and sweet spirit.

My Family & Friends: To those who have loved and supported me throughout my life – THANK YOU! Your investments in my growth journey were sources of encouragement that continue to help me evolve and flourish!

To Susan and Patty - Thank you for repeatedly helping me refine my manuscript. You both are so special to me, I'm grateful for your presence in my life.

Source References

"What Is Parentification? Signs of a Parentified Child", Newport Academy, December 20, 2022, NewportAcademy.com,

"President Obama's Fatherhood Speech", Politico, June 15, 2008, Politico. com,

"The Tony Evans Study Bible – Christian Standard Bible," By Tony Evans, Holmes Bible Publisher, Nashville, TN, 2017, Page 1385

"Crucial Conversation: Tools for Talking When Stakes are High," Second Edition, By Kerry Patterson, Joseph Grenny, Ron McMillan, Al Switzler, and Stephen R. Covey (Forward), McGraw-Hill Publishing, September 16, 2001,

About the Author

Fa'Shay (Raine) Halley is known for her passionate servant-leadership approach, which she invests in every role she's blessed with. However, the role she holds most dear to her heart is as a wife of more than 22 years to Darrell and mother to her young adult children Asia and Jaden. She has also enjoyed a successful career in leadership for more than 20 years at one of the world's largest financial institutions. As an active Alpha Kappa Alpha Sorority Inc. member, and through her corporate philanthropic efforts, Fa'Shay enjoys engaging in diverse community service opportunities.

As a graduate student with a concentration in "Educational Leadership," Fa'Shay has made it her mission to explore and maximize every opportunity to connect, encourage, educate, and elevate others. Her heart for restoring and building relationships set her on the path to writing this book. This book is a labor of love that was divinely inspired and paid homage to her Heavenly Father, Bonus Dads, husband, and the many Dads she learned from throughout her life.

Fa'Shay is a grateful learner and servant-leader determined to walk out her divine purpose and live life in full bloom while helping others do the same.

"When I stand before God at the end of my life, I would hope that I would not have a single bit of talent left, and could say, 'I used everything you gave me.'"
- CHADWICK BOSEMAN

Connect with the Author

Website: www.intentionaldadsmovement.com

Social Media:
Intentional Dads Movement – Instagram, FaceBook & YouTube

Email: IDMovement2020@gmail.com